NON SANZ DROICT.

William Shakespeare

THE
COMEDY OF ERRORS

**With New Dramatic Criticism
and an Updated Bibliography**

Edited by Harry Levin

The Signet Classic Shakespeare
GENERAL EDITOR: SYLVAN BARNET

A SIGNET CLASSIC

NEW AMERICAN LIBRARY

A DIVISION OF PENGUIN BOOKS USA INC., NEW YORK
PUBLISHED IN CANADA BY
PENGUIN BOOKS CANADA LIMITED, MARKHAM, ONTARIO

SIGNET, SIGNET CLASSIC, MENTOR, ONYX, PLUME, MERIDIAN AND
NAL BOOKS are published in the United States by
New American Library, a division of Penguin Books USA Inc.,
1633 Broadway, New York, New York 10019,
in Canada by Penguin Books Canada Limited,
2801 John Street, Markham, Ontario L3R 1B4

12   13   14   15   16   17   18   19   20

PRINTED IN THE UNITED STATES OF AMERICA

Table of Contents

Shakespeare: Prefatory Remarks

Between the record of his baptism in Stratford on 26 April 1564 and the record of his burial in Stratford on 25 April 1616, some forty documents name Shakespeare, and many others name his parents, his children, and his grandchildren. More facts are known about William Shakespeare than about any other playwright of the period except Ben Jonson. The facts should, however, be distinguished from the legends. The latter, inevitably more engaging and better known, tell us that the Stratford boy killed a calf in high style, poached deer and rabbits, and was forced to flee to London, where he held horses outside a playhouse. These traditions are only traditions; they may be true, but no evidence supports them, and it is well to stick to the facts.

Mary Arden, the dramatist's mother, was the daughter of a substantial landowner; about 1557 she married John Shakespeare, who was a glove-maker and trader in various farm commodities. In 1557 John Shakespeare was a member of the Council (the governing body of Stratford), in 1558 a constable of the borough, in 1561 one of the two town chamberlains, in 1565 an alderman (entitling him to the appellation "Mr."), in 1568 high bailiff—the town's highest political office, equivalent to mayor. After 1577, for an unknown reason he drops out of local politics. The birthday of William Shakespeare, the eldest son of this locally prominent man, is unrecorded; but the Stratford parish register records that the infant was baptized on 26 April 1564. (It is quite possible that he was born on 23

April, but this date has probably been assigned by tradition because it is the date on which, fifty-two years later, he died.) The attendance records of the Stratford grammar school of the period are not extant, but it is reasonable to assume that the son of a local official attended the school and received substantial training in Latin. The masters of the school from Shakespeare's seventh to fifteenth years held Oxford degrees; the Elizabethan curriculum excluded mathematics and the natural sciences but taught a good deal of Latin rhetoric, logic, and literature. On 27 November 1582 a marriage license was issued to Shakespeare and Anne Hathaway, eight years his senior. The couple had a child in May, 1583. Perhaps the marriage was necessary, but perhaps the couple had earlier engaged in a formal "troth plight" which would render their children legitimate even if no further ceremony were performed. In 1585 Anne Hathaway bore Shakespeare twins.

That Shakespeare was born is excellent; that he married and had children is pleasant; but that we know nothing about his departure from Stratford to London, or about the beginning of his theatrical career, is lamentable and must be admitted. We would gladly sacrifice details about his children's baptism for details about his earliest days on the stage. Perhaps the poaching episode is true (but it is first reported almost a century after Shakespeare's death), or perhaps he first left Stratford to be a schoolteacher, as another tradition holds; perhaps he was moved by

> Such wind as scatters young men through the world,
> To seek their fortunes further than at home
> Where small experience grows.

In 1592, thanks to the cantankerousness of Robert Greene, a rival playwright and a pamphleteer, we have our first reference, a snarling one, to Shakespeare as an actor and playwright. Greene warns those of his own educated friends who wrote for the theater against an actor who has presumed to turn playwright:

There is an upstart crow, beautified with our feathers,
that with his *tiger's heart wrapped in a player's hide* supposes he is as well able to bombast out a blank verse as
the best of you, and being an absolute Johannes-factotum
is in his own conceit the only Shake-scene in a country.

The reference to the player, as well as the allusion to
Aesop's crow (who strutted in borrowed plumage, as an
actor struts in fine words not his own), makes it clear
that by this date Shakespeare had both acted and written. That Shakespeare is meant is indicated not only by
"Shake-scene" but by the parody of a line from one of
Shakespeare's plays, *3 Henry VI:* "O, tiger's heart wrapped
in a woman's hide." If Shakespeare in 1592 was prominent enough to be attacked by an envious dramatist, he
probably had served an apprenticeship in the theater for
at least a few years.

In any case, by 1592 Shakespeare had acted and written, and there are a number of subsequent references to
him as an actor: documents indicate that in 1598 he is
a "principal comedian," in 1603 a "principal tragedian,"
in 1608 he is one of the "men players." The profession
of actor was not for a gentleman, and it occasionally drew
the scorn of university men who resented writing speeches
for persons less educated than themselves, but it was
respectable enough: players, if prosperous, were in effect
members of the bourgeoisie, and there is nothing to suggest that Stratford considered William Shakespeare less
than a solid citizen. When, in 1596, the Shakespeares
were granted a coat of arms, the grant was made to Shakespeare's father, but probably William Shakespeare (who
the next year bought the second-largest house in town)
had arranged the matter on his own behalf. In subsequent
transactions he is occasionally styled a gentleman.

Although in 1593 and 1594 Shakespeare published two
narrative poems dedicated to the Earl of Southampton,
Venus and Adonis and *The Rape of Lucrece,* and may
well have written most or all of his sonnets in the middle nineties, Shakespeare's literary activity seems to have
been almost entirely devoted to the theater. (It may be

significant that the two narrative poems were written in years when the plague closed the theaters for several months.) In 1594 he was a charter member of the theatrical company called the Chamberlain's Men (which in 1603 changed its name to the King's Men); until he retired to Stratford (about 1611, apparently), he was with this remarkably stable company. From 1599 the company acted primarily at the Globe Theatre, in which Shakespeare held a one-tenth interest. Other Elizabethan dramatists are known to have acted, but no other is known also to have been entitled to a share in the profits of the playhouse.

Shakespeare's first eight published plays did not have his name on them, but this is not remarkable; the most popular play of the sixteenth century, Thomas Kyd's *The Spanish Tragedy,* went through many editions without naming Kyd, and Kyd's authorship is known only because a book on the profession of acting happens to quote (and attribute to Kyd) some lines on the interest of Roman emperors in the drama. What is remarkable is that after 1598 Shakespeare's name commonly appears on printed plays—some of which are not his. Another indication of his popularity comes from Francis Meres, author of *Palladis Tamia: Wit's Treasury* (1598): in this anthology of snippets accompanied by an essay on literature, many playwrights are mentioned, but Shakespeare's name occurs more often than any other, and Shakespeare is the only playwright whose plays are listed.

From his acting, playwriting, and share in a theater, Shakespeare seems to have made considerable money. He put it to work, making substantial investments in Stratford real estate. When he made his will (less than a month before he died), he sought to leave his property intact to his descendants. Of small bequests to relatives and to friends (including three actors, Richard Burbage, John Heminges, and Henry Condell), that to his wife of the second-best bed has provoked the most comment; perhaps it was the bed the couple had slept in, the best being reserved for visitors. In any case, had Shakespeare not excepted it, the bed would have gone (with the rest

of his household possessions) to his daughter and her
husband. On 25 April 1616 he was buried within the
chancel of the church at Stratford. An unattractive monu-
ment to his memory, placed on a wall near the grave, says
he died on 23 April. Over the grave itself are the lines,
perhaps by Shakespeare, that (more than his literary fame)
have kept his bones undisturbed in the crowded burial
ground where old bones were often dislodged to make
way for new:

> Good friend, for Jesus' sake forbear
> To dig the dust enclosèd here.
> Blessed be the man that spares these stones
> And cursed be he that moves my bones.

Thirty-seven plays, as well as some nondramatic poems,
are held to constitute the Shakespeare canon. The dates
of composition of most of the works are highly uncertain,
but there is often evidence of a *terminus a quo* (starting
point) and/or a *terminus ad quem* (terminal point) that
provides a framework for intelligent guessing. For example,
Richard II cannot be earlier than 1595, the publication
date of some material to which it is indebted; *The Merchant of Venice* cannot be later than 1598, the year Francis
Meres mentioned it. Sometimes arguments for a date hang
on an alleged topical allusion, such as the lines about the
unseasonable weather in *A Midsummer Night's Dream*,
II.i.81–117, but such an allusion (if indeed it is an allusion) can be variously interpreted, and in any case there is
always the possibility that a topical allusion was inserted
during a revision, years after the composition of a play.
Dates are often attributed on the basis of style, and although conjectures about style usually rest on other conjectures, sooner or later one must rely on one's literary
sense. There is no real proof, for example, that *Othello* is
not as early as *Romeo and Juliet*, but one feels *Othello*
is later, and because the first record of its performance
is 1604, one is glad enough to set its composition at that
date and not push it back into Shakespeare's early years.
The following chronology, then, is as much indebted to

informed guesswork and sensitivity as it is to fact. The dates, necessarily imprecise, indicate something like a scholarly consensus.

PLAYS

1588–93	*The Comedy of Errors*
1588–94	*Love's Labor's Lost*
1590–91	*2 Henry VI*
1590–91	*3 Henry VI*
1591–92	*1 Henry VI*
1592–93	*Richard III*
1592–94	*Titus Andronicus*
1593–94	*The Taming of the Shrew*
1593–95	*The Two Gentlemen of Verona*
1594–96	*Romeo and Juliet*
1595	*Richard II*
1594–96	*A Midsummer Night's Dream*
1596–97	*King John*
1596–97	*The Merchant of Venice*
1597	*1 Henry IV*
1597–98	*2 Henry IV*
1598–99	*Henry V*
1598–1600	*Much Ado About Nothing*
1599	*Julius Caesar*
1599–1600	*As You Like It*
1599–1600	*Twelfth Night*
1600–01	*Hamlet*
1597–1601	*The Merry Wives of Windsor*
1601–02	*Troilus and Cressida*
1602–04	*All's Well That Ends Well*
1603–04	*Othello*
1604	*Measure for Measure*
1605–06	*King Lear*
1605–06	*Macbeth*
1606–07	*Antony and Cleopatra*
1605–08	*Timon of Athens*
1607–09	*Coriolanus*
1608–09	*Pericles*
1609–10	*Cymbeline*

1610–11	*The Winter's Tale*
1611	*The Tempest*
1612–13	*Henry VIII*

POEMS

1592	*Venus and Adonis*
1593–94	*The Rape of Lucrece*
1593–1600	*Sonnets*
1600–01	*The Phoenix and the Turtle*

Shakespeare's Theater

In Shakespeare's infancy, Elizabethan actors performed wherever they could—in great halls, at court, in the courtyards of inns. The innyards must have made rather unsatisfactory theaters: on some days they were unavailable because carters bringing goods to London used them as depots; when available, they had to be rented from the innkeeper; perhaps most important, London inns were subject to the Common Council of London, which was not well disposed toward theatricals. In 1574 the Common Council required that plays and playing places in London be licensed. It asserted that

> sundry great disorders and inconveniences have been found to ensue to this city by the inordinate haunting of great multitudes of people, specially youth, to plays, interludes, and shows, namely occasion of frays and quarrels, evil practices of incontinency in great inns having chambers and secret places adjoining to their open stages and galleries,

and ordered that innkeepers who wished licenses to hold performances put up a bond and make contributions to the poor.

The requirement that plays and innyard theaters be licensed, along with the other drawbacks of playing at inns, probably drove James Burbage (a carpenter-turned-actor) to rent in 1576 a plot of land northeast of the city walls and to build here—on property outside the jurisdiction of the city—England's first permanent construction designed for plays. He called it simply the Theatre. About all that is known of its construction is that it was wood. It soon had imitators, the most famous being the Globe (1599), built across the Thames (again outside the city's jurisdiction), out of timbers of the Theatre, which had been dismantled when Burbage's lease ran out.

There are three important sources of information about the structure of Elizabethan playhouses—drawings, a contract, and stage directions in plays. Of drawings, only the so-called De Witt drawing (c. 1596) of the Swan— really a friend's copy of De Witt's drawing—is of much significance. It shows a building of three tiers, with a stage jutting from a wall into the yard or center of the building. The tiers are roofed, and part of the stage is covered by a roof that projects from the rear and is supported at its front on two posts, but the groundlings, who paid a penny to stand in front of the stage, were exposed to the sky. (Performances in such a playhouse were held only in the daytime; artificial illumination was not used.) At the rear of the stage are two doors; above the stage is a gallery. The second major source of information, the contract for the Fortune, specifies that although the Globe is to be the model, the Fortune is to be square, eighty feet outside and fifty-five inside. The stage is to be forty-three feet broad, and is to extend into the middle of the yard (i.e., it is twenty-seven and a half feet deep). For patrons willing to pay more than the general admission charged of the groundlings, there were to be three galleries provided with seats. From the third chief source, stage directions, one learns that entrance to the stage was by doors, presumably spaced widely apart at the rear ("Enter one citizen at one door, and another at the other"), and that in addition to the platform stage there was occasionally some sort of curtained booth or alcove allowing for "discovery" scenes, and some sort of playing space "aloft" or "above" to represent (for example) the top of a city's walls or a room above the street. Doubtless each theater had its own peculiarities, but perhaps we can talk about a "typical" Elizabethan theater if we realize that no theater need exactly have fit the description, just as no father is the typical father with 3.7 children. This hypothetical theater is wooden, round or polygonal (in *Henry V* Shakespeare calls it a "wooden *O*"), capable of holding some eight hundred spectators standing in the yard around the projecting elevated stage and some fifteen hundred additional spectators seated in the three roofed galleries. The stage, protected by a "shadow" or "heavens" or roof, is entered by two doors; behind the doors is the "tiring house" (attiring house, i.e., dressing room), and above the doors is some sort of gallery that may sometimes hold spectators but that can be used (for example) as the bedroom from which Romeo—according to a stage direction in one text—"goeth down." Some evidence suggests that a throne can be lowered onto the platform stage, perhaps from the "shadow"; certainly characters can descend from the stage through a trap or traps into the cellar or "hell." Sometimes this space beneath the platform accommodates a sound-effects man or musician (in *Antony and Cleopatra* "music of the hautboys is under the stage") or an actor (in *Hamlet* the "Ghost cries under the stage"). Most characters simply walk on and off, but because there is no curtain in front of the platform, corpses will have to be carried off (Hamlet must lug Polonius' guts into the neighbor room), or will have to fall at the rear, where the curtain on the alcove or booth can be drawn to conceal them.

Such may have been the so-called "public theater." Another kind of theater, called the "private theater" because its much greater admission charge limited its audience to the wealthy or the prodigal, must be briefly mentioned. The private theater was basically a large room, entirely roofed and therefore artificially illuminated, with a stage at one end. In 1576 one such theater was established in Blackfriars, a Dominican priory in London that had been suppressed in 1538 and confiscated by the Crown and thus was not under the city's jurisdiction. All the actors in the Blackfriars theater were boys about eight to thirteen years old (in the public theaters similar boys played female parts; a boy Lady Macbeth played to a man Macbeth). This private theater had a precarious existence, and ceased operations in 1584. In 1596 James Burbage, who had already made theatrical history by building the Theatre, began to construct a second Blackfriars theater. He died in 1597, and for several years this second Blackfriars theater was used by a troupe of boys, but in 1608 two of Burbage's sons and five other actors (including Shakespeare) became joint operators of the theater, using it in the winter when the open-air Globe was unsuitable. Perhaps such a smaller theater, roofed, artificially illuminated, and with a tradition of a courtly audience, exerted an influence on Shakespeare's late plays.

Performances in the private theaters may well have had intermissions during which music was played, but in the public theaters the action was probably uninterrupted, flowing from scene to scene almost without a break. Actors would enter, speak, exit, and others would immediately enter and establish (if necessary) the new locale by a few properties and by words and gestures. Here are some samples of Shakespeare's scene painting:

> This is Illyria, lady.

> Well, this is the Forest of Arden.

> This castle hath a pleasant seat; the air
> Nimbly and sweetly recommends itself
> Unto our gentle senses.

On the other hand, it is a mistake to conceive of the Elizabethan stage as bare. Although Shakespeare's Chorus in *Henry V* calls the stage an "unworthy scaffold" and urges the spectators to "eke out our performance with your mind," there was considerable spectacle. The last act of *Macbeth*, for example, has five stage directions calling for "drum and colors," and another sort of appeal to the eye is indicated by the stage direction "Enter Mac-

duff, with Macbeth's head." Some scenery and properties
may have been substantial; doubtless a throne was used,
and in one play of the period we encounter this direction:
"Hector takes up a great piece of rock and casts at Ajax,
who tears up a young tree by the roots and assails Hector."
The matter is of some importance, and will be glanced
at again in the next section.

The Texts of Shakespeare

Though eighteen of his plays were published during
his lifetime, Shakespeare seems never to have supervised
their publication. There is nothing unusual here; when a
playwright sold a play to a theatrical company he sur-
rendered his ownership of it. Normally a company would
not publish the play, because to publish it meant to allow
competitors to acquire the piece. Some plays, however,
did get published: apparently treacherous actors sometimes pieced together a play for a publisher, sometimes a
company in need of money sold a play, and sometimes
a company allowed a play to be published that no longer
drew audiences. That Shakespeare did not concern himself with publication, then, is scarcely remarkable; of his
contemporaries only Ben Jonson carefully supervised the
publication of his own plays. In 1623, seven years after
Shakespeare's death, John Heminges and Henry Condell
(two senior members of Shakespeare's company, who had
performed with him for about twenty years) collected his
plays—published and unpublished—into a large volume,
commonly called the First Folio. (A folio is a volume
consisting of sheets that have been folded once, each sheet
thus making two leaves, or four pages. The eighteen plays
published during Shakespeare's lifetime had been issued
one play per volume in small books called quartos. Each
sheet in a quarto has been folded twice, making four
leaves, or eight pages.) The First Folio contains thirty-six
plays; a thirty-seventh, *Pericles*, though not in the Folio
is regarded as canonical. Heminges and Condell suggest
in an address "To the great variety of readers" that the

republished plays are presented in better form than in the quartos: "Before you were abused with diverse stolen and surreptitious copies, maimed and deformed by the frauds and stealths of injurious impostors that exposed them; even those, are now offered to your view cured and perfect of their limbs, and all the rest absolute in their numbers, as he [i.e., Shakespeare] conceived them."

Whoever was assigned to prepare the texts for publication in the First Folio seems to have taken his job seriously and yet not to have performed it with uniform care. The sources of the texts seem to have been, in general, good unpublished copies or the best published copies. The first play in the collection, *The Tempest,* is divided into acts and scenes, has unusually full stage directions and descriptions of spectacle, and concludes with a list of the characters, but the editor was not able (or willing) to present all of the succeeding texts so fully dressed. Later texts occasionally show signs of carelessness: in one scene of *Much Ado About Nothing* the names of actors, instead of characters, appear as speech prefixes, as they had in the quarto, which the Folio reprints; proofreading throughout the Folio is spotty and apparently was done without reference to the printer's copy; the pagination of *Hamlet* jumps from 156 to 257.

A modern editor of Shakespeare must first select his copy; no problem if the play exists only in the Folio, but a considerable problem if the relationship between a quarto and the Folio—or an early quarto and a later one—is unclear. When an editor has chosen what seems to him to be the most authoritative text or texts for his copy, he has not done with making decisions. First of all, he must reckon with Elizabethan spelling. If he is not producing a facsimile, he probably modernizes it, but ought he to preserve the old form of words that apparently were pronounced quite unlike their modern forms—"lanthorn," "alablaster"? If he preserves these forms, is he really preserving Shakespeare's forms or perhaps those of a compositor in the printing house? What is one to do when one finds "lanthorn" and "lantern" in adjacent lines? (The editors of this series in general, but not invariably, assume that words should be spelled in their modern form.) Elizabethan punctuation, too, presents problems. For example in the First Folio, the only text for the play, Macbeth rejects his wife's idea that he can wash the blood from his hand:

> no: this my Hand will rather
> The multitudinous Seas incarnadine,
> Making the Greene one, Red.

Obviously an editor will remove the superfluous capitals, and he will probably alter the spelling to "incarnadine," but will he leave the comma before "red," letting Macbeth speak of the sea as "the green one," or will he (like most modern editors) remove the comma and thus have Macbeth say that his hand will make the ocean *uniformly* red?

An editor will sometimes have to change more than spelling or punctuation. Macbeth says to his wife:

> I dare do all that may become a man,
> Who dares no more, is none.

For two centuries editors have agreed that the second line is unsatisfactory, and have emended "no" to "do": "Who dares do more is none." But when in the same play Ross says that fearful persons

> floate vpon a wilde and violent Sea
> Each way, and moue,

need "move" be emended to "none," as it often is, on the hunch that the compositor misread the manuscript? The editors of the Signet Classic Shakespeare have restrained themselves from making abundant emendations. In their minds they hear Dr. Johnson on the dangers of emending: "I have adopted the Roman sentiment, that it is more honorable to save a citizen than to kill an enemy." Some departures (in addition to spelling, punctuation, and lineation) from the copy text have of course been made, but the original readings are listed in a note following the play, so that the reader can evaluate them for himself.

The editors of the Signet Classic Shakespeare, following tradition, have added line numbers and in many cases act and scene divisions as well as indications of locale at the beginning of scenes. The Folio divided most of the plays into acts and some into scenes. Early eighteenth-century editors increased the divisions. These divisions, which provide a convenient way of referring to passages in the plays, have been retained, but when not in the text chosen as the basis for the Signet Classic text they are enclosed in square brackets [ ] to indicate that they are editorial additions. Similarly, although no play of Shakespeare's published during his lifetime was equipped with indications of locale at the heads of scene divisions, locales have here been added in square brackets for the convenience of the reader, who lacks the information afforded to spectators by costumes, properties, and gestures. The spectator can tell at a glance he is in the throne room, but without an editorial indication the reader may be puzzled for a while. It should be mentioned, incidentally, that there are a few authentic stage directions—perhaps Shakespeare's, perhaps a prompter's—that suggest locales: for example, "Enter Brutus in his orchard," and "They go up into the Senate house." It is hoped that the bracketed additions provide the reader with the sort of help provided in these two authentic directions, but it is equally hoped that the reader will remember that the stage was not loaded with scenery.

No editor during the course of his work can fail to recollect some words Heminges and Condell prefixed to the Folio:

> It had been a thing, we confess, worthy to have been wished, that the author himself had lived to have set forth and overseen his own writings. But since it hath been ordained otherwise, and he by death departed from that right, we pray you do not envy his friends the office of their care and pain to have collected and published them.

Nor can an editor, after he has done his best, forget Heminges and Condell's final words: "And so we leave you to other of his friends, whom if you need can be your guides. If you need them not, you can lead yourselves, and others. And such readers we wish him."

SYLVAN BARNET
Tufts University

Introduction

The Comedy of Errors has come down to us solely through the First Folio, in a good text which seems not far removed from the author's manuscript, and which is particularly interesting for the explicitness of its stage directions. The play itself is the shortest, and may indeed be the earliest, of Shakespeare's dramatic works. As such, it is more explicitly linked to classical tradition than any of the others. In spite of a notorious gibe by Ben Jonson, it is quite evident that Shakespeare was acquainted with certain standard Latin authors. There is even an accredited rumor that, before entering the theater, he had taught in a country school, where the curriculum would have consisted of very little else. If he was to assay the range of the repertory, Seneca could not be "too heavy," in the phrase of Polonius, "nor Plautus too light." *Titus Andronicus* was Shakespeare's early experiment in the mode of Senecan tragedy; *The Comedy of Errors* marks, rather more happily, his assimilation and extension of Plautine comedy. In that case there was a specific model, the archetypal comedy of twins, the *Menaechmi* or *Two Menaechmuses*. A lively translation into Elizabethan prose by one W.W. (who is commonly identified as the minor poet, William Warner) was published in 1595, some 1800 years after the appearance of Plautus' play on the Roman stage.

Whether Shakespeare could have seen an unpublished draft of this version, or whether W.W. was indebted to Shakespeare's free adaptation, has been argued back and forth by scholars. Certainly Shakespeare could have known the original at first hand, and the similar phrases used by both writers may be coincidences rather than echoes. At all events, the English *Menaechmi* offers a helpful basis of comparison whereby readers may observe for themselves how Shakespeare adapted and amplified Plautus. Such observations might well begin with W.W.'s title page: "A pleasant and fine Conceited Comedy taken out of the most excellent witty Poet Plautus, chosen purposely from out the rest as least harmful and yet delightful . . ." In other words, both the translator and the playwright chose to work from an untypical play—untypical in its all but complete reliance on chance and not on contrivance, not on malice or mischief but sheer luck. Not that fortune, often in the most commercial sense, was ever slow to intervene in the world of Greco-Roman comedy. But it was commonly sought through the profit motive on the part of the old, or sexual appetite on the part of the young, and the resultant conflicts were perennially exploited by parasites and abetted by slaves. Whereas tragedy took place in temples and palaces, the comic sphere was a round of urban shops and middle-class domiciles.

In the ancient theater the proscenium was not a picture frame but an architectural facade, whose practical doors and upper windows gave a stylized impression of a street scene in some Mediterranean seaport. By convention the side exits led to the marketplace in one direction (Shakespeare's Mart) and to the harbor in the other ("from the Bay"). Between them flowed the continual traffic of characters, pausing at one doorway or another to transact their business, and incidentally to inform the audience of the goings-on within. What Shakespeare calls "the stirring passage of the day" moved all the faster because it did not look beyond external appearances. Drama becomes more serious when it stresses characterization; farce, at the other extreme, tends to subordinate character to plot. Hence the *donnée* of Plautus was the very essence of the farcical: two characters sufficiently alike, so that each might fit interchangeably into the other's situation, could not afford to possess distinguishing characteristics. They are, by definition, altogether exceptional. In general, the *dramatis personae* of New Comedy—the kind of comedy that was new with Menander, yet was by no means exhausted with Molière—are stock types rather than fully characterized individuals. With many changes of costume and scenery, they continue to present object lessons in avarice, flattery, braggadocio, and other continuing deviations from sound morality.

Comedy, as Sir Philip Sidney defined it for Shakespeare's age, is "an imitation of the common errors of our life," which are represented "in the most ridiculous and scornful sort that may be, so as it is impossible that any beholder can be content to be such a one." Sidney, who was involved in the defense of poetry, may bear down too heavily for our taste upon the posture of dramatist as moralist; yet, in emphasizing the correction of error, he shifts to the enlightenment of the spectator and to that civilized overview which—through a process of confusion and clarification—we finally attain: "There, but for the grace of God, go we!" To err is proverbially human; and our tragic heroes go astray grandly by committing some single and fatal mistake. Comic figures, on the other hand, run through a whole train of petty errors, and somehow manage to extricate themselves from the final consequences. Hence it is not surprising that Shakespeare's generic title had its lost forerunners, notably a *History of Error* performed in 1577. It is recorded, too, that a gala performance of the Shakespearean *Comedy of Errors* was played by the legal gentlemen of Gray's Inn during the Christmas season of 1594 (probably two or three years after it was first publicly produced), with such crowds and attendant confusions that the festive occasion "was ever afterwards called *The Night of Errors*."

In his massive studies of Shakespeare's modest Latinity, T. W. Baldwin has shown that the poet may well have studied Plautus in the contemporaneous edition of Lambinus. There the text of the *Menaechmus* was flanked by a commentary in which each successive twist or turn of the plot is signalized by the Latin verb *errare* or the noun *error*. Thus the key word utilized by Shakespeare would seem to have had the force of a technical term. Along with it we may consider another term, introduced by that versatile literary innovator, George Gascoigne, through his English rendering of Ariosto's prose comedy, *The Supposes*. Now a "suppose," as Gascoigne defined it and applied it through a series of marginal comments on the action of the play, is "a mistaking or imagination of one thing for another," generally one person supposed to be someone else because of deception, disguise, or impersonation. It requires no plotting or counterplotting in a Machiavellian sense; the only plotter is Shakespeare or Plautus himself; and what he hatches is fobbed off upon us as a trick of fate, a freak of nature, a practical joke conceived and executed by providence. The misapprehensions that gave rise to it are not poses nor supposes nor impostures; they are, plainly and simply, errors. We are at the roulette table, not the chessboard, here.

Where tragedy individualizes its protagonists, comedy underscores those broad resemblances which make it difficult to tell people apart. The closer the similarity between them, the easier it becomes for us to confound them. Blunders are most easily committed when two differing alternatives closely resemble one another, though the resemblance be no more than skin-deep. "Two faces that are alike," Pascal remarked, "though neither of them excites laughter in itself, make me laugh when together on account of the likeness." It was this sentence of Pascal's that Bergson developed into his theory of laughter as a protest of the natural and the humane against all attempts at mechanization and regimentation. Duplication, in particular, seems an affront to human dignity (one is almost tempted to call it a loss of face)—to be always mistaken for, to be almost indistinguishable from, somebody else. A set of identical twins, leading different lives, is a possibility but not a probability; and Coleridge would invoke that classic distinction to draw a line between comedy and farce. Upon his recommendation we entertain the initial hypothesis; we verily believe it because it is absurd; for, after all, absurdity is man's lot as the Existentialists have redefined it. Plautus offered Shakespeare a basic theme for the unforced interplay of cross-purposes. Shakespeare's variations, widely echoed in their turn, would be blithely syncopated by Rodgers and Hart in their appealing musical comedy, *The Boys from Syracuse*.

The improbable assumption of Plautus was complicated to the very limits of the possible when Shakespeare dared to redouble the twins, and thereby to provide his pair of protagonists with a brace of retainers. Here he was acting on a hint from another Plautine source, a play so frequently imitated that Jean Giraudoux could number his treatment *Amphitryon 38*. Its myth is that of Alcmena, wooed by Jupiter in the shape of her absent husband Amphitryon, while Jupiter's companion, Mercury, assumes the person of Sosia, the household slave. Two of Shakespeare's most effective scenes, where the homecoming master and man are turned away from their own threshold, are directly inspired by Plautus' *Amphitryon*. Consequently, since each of Shakespeare's masters has a bond-servant, he does not need to attach an officious parasite to the local Menaechmus as Plautus does. Messenio, the clever servant who accompanies the Syracusan Menaechmus, warns him with a pun against Epidamnum, where no one escapes *"sine damno* (without damage)"; but the Epidamnian pitfalls turn out to be unsolicited favors, which the visitor accepts with increasing insouciance. As for the citizen-twin, he is a solid man of affairs; but, having had a falling-out with his wife (and Plautus wastes no sympathy whatsoever upon the shrewish Uxor or Roman matron), he sets aside the day's business for a night's pleasure. In the true holiday spirit, both brothers are on the town.

Shakespeare, in amplifying the wife's role, reduced the part assigned to the Courtesan. The pivotal banquet is served not at her hangout, the Porpentine, but at the home of Antipholus above his shop, the Phoenix; while he, a normally faithful husband, seeks out her company only after he has reason to suspect his wife. The latter, Adriana, inherits the Uxor's misunderstanding with her husband; but Shakespeare sublimates it to a plane of genuine, if too possessive, conjugal love. Moreover, he endows her with a sister, to be courted by the bachelor

Antipholus; and Luciana proves to be a *raisonneuse,* a mouthpiece of moderation, so that the twins occupy a place in the great Shakespearean debate on marriage, along with Kate and Petruchio or Rosaline and Berowne or Beatrice and Benedick. Shakespeare's characters live, as usual, in a Christian ethos. The perplexed traveler swears, "as I am a Christian," and—approached by the Courtesan—echoes Christ bidding Satan avaunt. The change in the ethical climate may be noted by the shift from Epidamnum, which is nonetheless mentioned along the way, to Ephesus. Plautus' Syracusans fear Epidamnum because it is an emporium of sharp practice, peopled by rogues and harlots and the usual comic types. Shakespeare's Syracusans are cautious too. "They say this town is full of cozenage," the traveling Antipholus warns himself.

Notwithstanding, the Ephesians he meets are not "disguised cheaters." They are, as the traveling Dromio puts it, "a gentle nation," who "speak us fair, give us gold." Shakespeare is more in his milieu where the setting is a room in the palace—or, better still, another part of the forest—than in the mercantile zones of New Comedy. It is not coney-catching but witchcraft and sorcery that envelop Ephesus in its mysterious aura. "Here we wander in illusions." This is a place of strangers and sojourners, given to curious arts, to echo the patron saint of travelers *in partibus infidelium,* the Apostle Paul. Not without pertinence, it has been suggested that Paul's Epistle to the Ephesians, with its injunctions for husbands and wives, and for servants and masters, may have been in the background of Shakespeare's mind. His far-flung romance of *Pericles,* based on the folk tale of Apollonius of Tyre as retold by John Gower, reaches its resolution in the famous Temple of Diana at Ephesus. Some of the elements of the late play are present in the early one, notably the vicissitudes of a family progressing through misadventure by sea to recognition under religious auspices. The pagan temple has its counterpart in the Priory, where—instead of a goddess in the machine—the flesh-and-blood Abbess is revealed to be the long-lost wife and mother.

The framing figure of Egeon contributes an emotional tension, at the very outset, to what would otherwise have remained a two-dimensional drama. His protracted expository narration is enlivened by the awareness that it is a plea, and probably a vain one, for his life. Rightly he blames his misfortunes on hap; for nowhere else in Shakespeare can a whole pattern of incidents be so directly traceable to sheer unmitigated contingency. Egeon is hopeless and helpless because he is hapless. But this is not to be a novel by Thomas Hardy; it is a knockabout farce, where bad fortune will change soon enough into good. The next scene not only offers a hint that the new arrival is one of Egeon's sons—through the mix-up of the Dromios—and that the other son is just around the corner, but virtually guarantees the ransom, since the sum mentioned in both scenes is exactly a thousand marks. Coincidence has already done its best, as well as its worst, and a happy ending has been implicit from the beginning. Meanwhile the sequence of farcical episodes has been framed by the tragicomic overplot; and Shakespeare, by enlisting our sympathies for the fate of Egeon, has charged the air with a suspense which cannot be resolved until the appointed hour of execution, five o'clock in the afternoon.

Both of the Antipholuses have appointments at that hour, one of them with the Merchant and the other with Angelo the Goldsmith; and since it is noon when the Syracusan arrives, and since the Ephesian Dromio gets into his troubles over the question of dinnertime, the time scheme is firmly fixed within the course of the afternoon. There are frequent reminders of time passing, to reinforce the structure of occurrences: when Komisarjevsky produced the play at Stratford-on-Avon, his setting was dominated by a gigantic clock. Adhering to the classical unities as Shakespeare does just once again in *The Tempest,* he takes the traditional city street as his horizon, moving his characters back and forth from port to Mart and in and out of the various doorways between. The play would seem to lend itself very conveniently to the simultaneous stage of a great hall, such as that of Gray's Inn, where three or four free-standing houses or so-called mansions would have corresponded to the labeled locations: the Phoenix, the Porpentine for the Courtesan, the Centaur inn, and the ultimate abbey near the place of execution. On the other hand, the recent production at Stratford, Ontario, demonstrated how well the play could adapt to the multilevel mobility of an Elizabethan playhouse.

The problem of staging ought not to be unduly strained by the presupposition that calls for identical twins. To be sure, the difficulty raised by the twins of two sexes in *Twelfth Night,* which would have been solved in Shakespeare's day when both parts were acted by young men, is virtually insoluble in the modern theater. But, granted an approximate equivalence of stature, plus the same costuming and make-up, the Antipholuses and Dromios ought to look enough alike to confuse the other characters without confusing the audience. Is it not our premise, in viewing a comedy, that we are brighter than those who are on the stage? In the Roman theater, where the employment of masks eliminated the facial disparities, Plautus had to give a tassel to Mercury and a feather to Jupiter so that they would not be confused with Sosia and Amphitryon. At Stratford, Connecticut, in 1963, the same actor was cast as both twins, thereby combining histrionic virtuosity with artistic economy. This directorial tactic must create a bigger dilemma than the one it endeavors to solve, since the audience can never know the moment of catharsis, the visual illumination of seeing the two confusing elements discriminated from one another and exhibited side by side.

That way schizophrenia lies—which does not mean that it would be unproduceable in the Theater of the Absurd. It might turn out to be something in the vein of Pirandello, if not a dramatization of *Dr. Jekyll and Mr. Hyde.* But the actual predicament is that of two personalities forced into the same role, rather than that of one personality playing two roles, since the resident twin has the contacts and continuities, and the roving twin intercepts them, as it were. Tweedledum has got to match Tweedledee, more or less, in order to be taken for him; and yet, the less he feels like him, the more the dramatic irony. Plautus did not discriminate between his two very sharply; the discrepancies that emerged largely took the concrete form of objects which fell into the wrong hands; otherwise the interconnecting characters did not seem to notice much difference. The married Menaechmus was angry from the first, so that each new chagrin could be rationalized to his mood. The interloping Menaechmus, though considerably bewildered, had no cause for being dissatisfied with his reception. Neither of them was above the temptation to profit from the contretemps; and the interloper finally engaged in a stratagem of his own, when he joined the game and pretended to be a lunatic.

That sort of conduct is what we have agreed to label a suppose, a deception which is cultivated rather than casual. The most notable fact about Shakespeare's comedy is that it has no supposes, only errors: only mischances, and no contrivances by anybody except Shakespeare himself. There is no parallel scene of pretended madness; Shakespeare must have been saving the theme for *Hamlet*. Here the suspected madman, like Malvolio in *Twelfth Night*, protests his sanity. He does not act; he is acted upon; and Shakespeare, ever the psychologist, makes a good deal more out of the attempted diagnosis of demonic possession. He makes the exorcism so very painful, and goes so far out of his way to substitute the grim-visaged schoolmaster, Dr. Pinch, for the Plautine Medicus that we sense a virtual obsession, possibly connected with Holofernes, the pedant of *Love's Labor's Lost,* or with some other reminiscence from Shakespeare's own teaching days. It is as if the nightmare came so close that the misunderstood hero dare not pretend to be hallucinated. Again there is a precedent in Saint Paul's Epistle to the Ephesians, where the exorcist is exorcised. The customary rhetorical questions of comedy, in these mouths, become questions of existential bewilderment or expressions of cosmic vertigo: Do I dream or wake? Do we see double? Is he drunk or sober? Is she a liar or a fool? Who is crazy? Who is sane?

Contrasted with this constant inner questioning, the caricature of Dr. Pinch seems externalized. He is the one humorous personage of the play, in the Jonsonian usage, a man of obvious quirks and eccentric aspect, the crazy psychiatrist. If the others are funny, it is because of the plights they find themselves in. No, there is one other exception, though she is peripheral, and has a greater impact in her absence than in her presence onstage. This heroine, invoked indifferently as Luce or Nell, is generically a Dowsabel or, for that matter, a Dulcinea—a kitchen maid whose formidable proportions are vividly verbalized by the wrong Dromio, her brother-in-law, who is still quaking from the shock of having been claimed by her as a husband. This is the vulgar parallel to Adriana's claim upon her brother-in-law. Dromio's description of his brother's Nell, elicited by his master's queries as straight man, is a set-piece in the manner of Launce or Launcelot Gobbo, and may well have been assigned to the same comedian. With its geographical conceits, comparing the parts of her person to foreign countries (and containing, incidentally, the sole direct allusion that Shakespeare makes to America), it might almost be a ribald reversal of Othello's traveler's tales when wooing Desdemona.

But it is by no means a far-fetched gag, since it embodies—on a more than miniature scale—the principal contrast of the play: on the one hand, extensive voyaging; on the other, intensive domesticity. In using an underplot which burlesques the main plot, Shakespeare employs a device as old as Medwall's pioneer interlude of *Fulgens and Lucres,* where the rival suitors have servants who court the mistress' maid under the diagrammatic designations of A and B. With Nell, as with the demanding Adriana, the normal approaches of courtship are reversed. The closest we come to romantic love is the sketchy relationship between her brother-in-law and her husband's sister-in-law. Yet that is a good deal closer than Plautus brings us; and though both masters are suitably mated in the end, the concluding dialogue of the servants emphasizes the pairing of twins, not spouses. Parents and children are re-

united, family ties are reasserted; but Dromio of Syracuse
remains a free agent. His greatest moment has been the
midpoint of the play, when he acted as doorkeeper and
kept out his fellow Dromio, as well as that Dromio's
master, the master of the house. This is the one point
before the denouement when Shakespeare permits his
twins to meet and talk, and the door between them seems
to keep the mutual visibility fairly obscure.

It is worth noting that their brief colloquy reverts to
the doggerel style of *Ralph Roister Doister,* the oldest
English imitation of Plautus, in its stichomythic inter-
changes of rhyming fourteeners. This is the main scene
(the first of Act III) that Shakespeare borrowed from the
Amphitryon (the first of Act I), eking out the comedy of
the *Menaechmi* with the underplot of the two Sosias to
complete—with a vengeance—the Elizabethan requirements for a double plot. He develops it to the very pitch
of the dramatic subversion that he has been exploiting,
with the outsider inside and the insider excluded, the
stranger in possession of the house and the householder
cast into outer darkness. Both parties are translated, as
Quince will affirm of Bottom; and they could not have
been so completely translated, had they not been facsimiles to begin with. The most fundamental alteration
that Shakespeare made in his Plautine material was to
shift the focus from the homekeeping twin to his errant
brother, whose sobriquet, Antipholus Erotes, may be a
variation on Erratus or Errans. The *Menaechmi* starts
out with the other twin, and with the reassurance of
familiar surroundings, into which the disturbing factor
will be injected. *The Comedy of Errors* starts with the
newcomer, and his impressions of strangeness: the witch-
ery of Ephesus, not the bustle of Epidamnum.

Having a head start, and having to alternate scenes with
Antipholus of Ephesus who does not appear until the
third act, Antipholus of Syracuse has a much larger part:
roughly 272 lines to the other's 207. The disproportion
is even clearer between the parts of the two Dromios:
there the score is Syracuse 233, Ephesus 162. The
Menaechmi, though it is the shorter play, has fewer char-

acters and longer speeches; accordingly, its Syracusan twin has 251 lines, whereas the Epidamnian twin has 300. We therefore tend to visualize what goes on in the Latin play from the denizen's standpoint, and what goes on in the English play from the alien's. Epidamnum could be any old town, where everything should be in its place, *in situ:* where everyone expects his fellow citizen, Menaechmus, to go through the round of his habitual day. No one could suspect that there was another Menaechmus, whose chance encounters would lead to incongruities and discontinuities, except for his one follower, who shares and compounds his perplexities. Ephesus is another story, however. We are put off at once by the hostile reception of Egeon; and when the two other foreigners enter, Antipholus and Dromio, they are the first of those names whom we have met.

We share their misgivings all the more readily because they too have been risking their lives, and because the object of their travels has so far eluded them. When this Antipholus gets caught up in his brother's existence, it is as new to us as it is to him. We participate in an adventure; what might be matter-of-fact to an Ephesian is, for him and ourselves, a fantasy out of the *Arabian Nights*. "What error drives our eyes and ears amiss?" he wonders, after Adriana accosts him, reprimands him, and invites him to dinner. And tentatively he resolves,

> Until I know this sure uncertainty,
> I'll entertain the offered fallacy.

Then, after dinner, smitten with Luciana, he asks her to unfold the mystery:

> Teach me, dear creature, how to think and speak:
> Lay open to my earthy-gross conceit,
> Smoth'red in errors, feeble, shallow, weak,
> The folded meaning of your words' deceit.

But the undeception does not come about until all the participants in this "sympathizèd one day's error"—for so the Abbess sums it up—have sought the illumination of sanctuary within her abbey. In that cloistered serenity, far from urban corruption, the deferred recognition scenes can coincide at long last. The confessions and counter-accusations piece together a step-by-step recapitulation of how "these errors are arose." The maternal figure of the Abbess is something of a surprise, as Bertrand Evans points out in his analytic study, *Shakespeare's Comedies*. Running through all of them, Mr. Evans finds their common structural principle in what he calls a "discrepant awareness." Characteristically, the humor springs from "the exploitable gulf spread between the participants' understanding and ours."

In Shakespeare's development of this resource, *The Comedy of Errors* is primordial, since it is his single comedy where the audience knows all and all the characters are in the dark. Mr. Evans' suggestive analysis can be perfectly fitted to the *Menaechmi*. Plautus, in effect, is always saying, "I told you so." But Shakespeare is always asking, "Can such things be?" The exceptional position of the Abbess not only rounds out the recognitions; it lays the spell of wonderment again upon the concluding scene; and it reminds us, as other touches do, of Shakespeare's romances. Even within the venal and angular precincts of Latinate Comedy, he can make us aware of unpathed waters, undreamed shores, and things in heaven and earth that philosophy has not fathomed. Yet philosophers can tell us much, particularly about the processes of learning; and Bergson tells us much about *The Comedy of Errors* when, in his essay on laughter, he borrows a concept from optics and writes of "the reciprocal interference of series." At length we can put our supposes or errors down in scientific terminology. "A situation is invariably comic," Bergson explains, "when it belongs simultaneously to two independent series of events, and is capable of being interpreted in two entirely different meanings at the same time."

It would be hard to conceive of a better illustration than the two different series of events in the respective days of the two Antipholuses, and the ways in which they are imperceptibly crisscrossed. Antipholus of Syracuse has no particular expectations or plans. He derives a gratuitous enjoyment from the inexplicable services rendered and favors due his brother. This interference or substitution induces a certain amnesia on the brother's part, when the bills come in and the witnesses testify; naturally, he cannot remember the items attested. As one error engenders another, suspicion is bound to mount and disgruntlement spread, rising to their climax in hot pursuit toward the madhouse or the jail, and ending at the Priory. Now the brunt of these displacements is borne by Antipholus of Ephesus. Of all those discomfited, he comes nearest to being a victim of the situation, since it is his situation, in the last analysis. It is his routine which is broken up, his standing in the community undermined; his normal expectations are interfered with, and—to add insult to injury—he is expected to pay for what he has been deprived of. In short, the rug has been pulled out from under the very preconditions of his existence.

Other people's bafflement can be fun, and Plautus makes the most of it. From the heights of our spectatorial vantage point, we need not worry too much about what befalls whom. We are not playing blind man's buff, we are watching the game. But Shakespeare makes us feel what it is like to be this or that Antipholus—all the difference in the world, if we happened to start by being the other one—and the interaction of opposite numbers ends by demonstrating *a fortiori* the uniqueness of the individual. When Adriana and her husband appeal to the Duke, the stories they tell of their day's experience are mutually contradictory; but the discrepancies would disappear if the shadow of the interfering Antipholus were retraced through their reciprocal patterns. (Latter-day readers or viewers may be reminded of the Japanese story or film, *Rashomon*.) It has been a lesson for Adriana, brought home by the gentle rebuke of the Abbess, and penitently acknowledged. For Antipholus of Ephesus, it has been an eye-opening misadventure. Apparently, he has never felt the impetus that has incited his brother and his father to sally forth in search of him. Unconcerned

ith his foundling origin, he rejoices in the good graces
f the Duke and takes for granted the stable comforts of
is Ephesian citizenship.

What greater shock for him, then, than to bring a party
f fellow citizens home to his well-established household
or lunch and to discover that household preempted by
oistering strangers, to be shut out in the street, to have
ne's own door slammed in one's own face? Or is it one's
wn? The sense of alienation, that *Verfremdungseffekt* so
haracteristic of Brecht and of the twentieth-century the-
ter, is all the greater when our image of ourselves de-
ends for its corroboration upon a settled context, and
hen we come to realize—what tragedy teaches us—that
: is our destiny to be displaced. When Messenio saw the
vo Menaechmuses together, he declared that water was
ot more like water. After Shakespeare has adapted the
netaphor, it stands not for an easy correspondence but
or an unending quest.

> I to the world am like a drop of water
> That in the ocean seeks another drop,

ntipholus of Syracuse confesses sadly, realizing that he
s less likely to find a mother and a brother than to be
rretrievably lost himself. Later, Adriana, addressing him
s if he were Antipholus of Ephesus, likens their imperiled
ove to a drop of water into the sea; and he has a similar
xchange with Luciana. The Syracusan twin is conscious
hat he must lose his identity in order to find it; the
phesian twin is not; but he must, and he does. And
)romio too—both Dromios, whichever is which—must
ndergo their crises of identity: "Am I Dromio? Am I
our man? Am I myself?"

Modern psychological fiction is haunted by doubles,
ometimes as overtly as in the tales of Hoffmann, Poe,
nd Dostoevsky, or in "The Jolly Corner" of Henry
ames, where the Black Stranger is recognized as the
elf that might have been. The other self—best friend,
vorst enemy—stares back at the poets from Heine's pallid
host (*"Du! Doppelgänger, du bleicher Geselle!"*) or

Baudelaire's hypocritical reader (*"mon semblable! mo frère!"*). That alter ego may be demon or devil, goo angel or evil genius. It may be the retribution of cor science—Philip Drunk reprehended by Philip Sober—or at the other extreme, the vicarious pleasure the artist er joys through the playboy, the envy of Shem for Shau All this may well be a far cry from Plautine or eve Shakespearean farce, to which we should be glad that w can escape from our more introspective dilemmas. The all aberrations come home to roost, and are sorted out b the happy ending; we acknowledge the error of our way and false suppositions are replaced by truths. No or really gets damaged in Epidamnum, and everyone enjoy a new lease of life when Egeon is ransomed and reprieve Everything will be explained at a feast, after the conver tional manner of comedy. Debts will be paid, relation ships renewed, and daily routine taken up where it brok off. Having been restored once more to our familiar worl we laugh away the shudder of estrangement.

HARRY LEVI
Harvard Universi

The Comedy of Errors

The Comedy of Errors

ACT I

Scene I. [*A public place.*]

Enter the Duke of Ephesus, with [Egeon] the Merchant of Syracusa,°[1] *Jailer, and other Attendants.*

Egeon. Proceed, Solinus, to procure my fall,
And by the doom° of death end woes and all.

Duke. Merchant of Syracusa, plead no more;
I am not partial° to infringe our laws.
The enmity and discord which of late   5
Sprung from the rancorous outrage of your Duke
To merchants, our well-dealing countrymen,
Who, wanting guilders° to redeem their lives,
Have sealed his rigorous statutes with their bloods,
Excludes all pity from our threat'ning looks.   10
For, since the mortal and intestine jars°
'Twixt thy seditious countrymen and us,

---

[1] The degree sign (°) indicates a footnote, which is keyed to the text by line number. Text references are printed in **boldface** type; the annotation follows in roman type.

I.i.s.d. Syracusa Syracuse, ancient capital of Sicily   **2 doom** sentence   **4 partial** predisposed   **8 guilders** Dutch coins worth about forty cents   **11 intestine jars** internal conflicts

It hath in solemn synods been decreed,
Both by the Syracusians and ourselves,
15 To admit no traffic to our adverse° towns.
Nay more; if any born at Ephesus°
Be seen at Syracusian marts and fairs;
Again, if any Syracusian born
Come to the bay of Ephesus, he dies,
20 His goods confiscate to the Duke's dispose,°
Unless a thousand marks° be levièd
To quit° the penalty and to ransom him.
Thy substance, valued at the highest rate,
Cannot amount unto a hundred marks;
25 Therefore by law thou art condemned to die.

Egeon. Yet this my comfort: when your words are
    done,
My woes end likewise with the evening sun.

Duke. Well, Syracusian, say, in brief, the cause
Why thou departed'st from thy native home,
30 And for what cause thou cam'st to Ephesus.

Egeon. A heavier task could not have been imposed
Than I to speak my griefs unspeakable;
Yet, that the world may witness that my end
Was wrought by nature, not by vile offense,
35 I'll utter what my sorrow gives me leave.
In Syracusa was I born, and wed
Unto a woman happy but for me,
And by me, had not our hap been bad.
With her I lived in joy, our wealth increased
40 By prosperous voyages I often made
To Epidamnum,° till my factor's° death
And the great care of goods at random left
Drew me from kind embracements of my spouse;
From whom my absence was not six months old,
45 Before herself—almost at fainting under
The pleasing punishment that women bear—

15 **adverse** hostile   16 **Ephesus** (rich city on the coast of Asia Minor)
20 **dispose** disposal   21 **marks** (valued at somewhat more than three
dollars)   22 **quit** acquit   41 **Epidamnum** (Adriatic seaport)   41 **factor's** agent's

Had made provision for her following me,
And soon and safe arrivèd where I was.
There had she not been long, but she became
A joyful mother of two goodly sons;   50
And, which was strange, the one so like the other,
As could not be distinguished but by names.
That very hour, and in the self-same inn,
A mean° woman was deliverèd
Of such a burden male, twins both alike.   55
Those, for° their parents were exceeding poor,
I bought, and brought up to attend my sons.
My wife, not meanly° proud of two such boys,
Made daily motions° for our home return.
Unwilling I agreed; alas, too soon   60
We came aboard.
A league from Epidamnum had we sailed
Before the always wind-obeying deep
Gave any tragic instance° of our harm.
But longer did we not retain much hope;   65
For what obscurèd light the heavens did grant
Did but convey unto our fearful minds
A doubtful warrant° of immediate death,
Which, though myself would gladly have embraced,
Yet the incessant weepings of my wife,   70
Weeping before for what she saw must come,
And piteous plainings° of the pretty babes,
That mourned for fashion,° ignorant what to fear,
Forced me to seek delays for them and me.
And this it was—for other means was none: 75
The sailors sought for safety by our boat,
And left the ship, then sinking-ripe,° to us.
My wife, more careful for the latter-born,°
Had fast'ned him unto a small spare mast,
Such as seafaring men provide for storms;   80
To him one of the other twins was bound,
Whilst I had been like heedful of the other.

54 mean poor   56 for because   58 not meanly more than a little
59 motions proposals   64 instance token   68 doubtful warrant om-
inous sign   72 plainings wails   73 fashion custom   77 sinking-ripe
ready to sink   78 latter-born (but see line 124)

The children thus disposed, my wife and I,
Fixing our eyes on whom our care was fixed,
85 Fast'ned ourselves at either end the mast;
And floating straight, obedient to the stream,
Was carried towards Corinth,° as we thought.
At length the sun, gazing upon the earth,
Dispersed those vapors that offended us,
90 And, by the benefit of his wishèd° light,
The seas waxed calm, and we discoverèd
Two ships from far, making amain° to us:
Of Corinth that, of Epidaurus° this.
But ere they came—O, let me say no more!
95 Gather the sequel by that went before.

Duke. Nay, forward, old man; do not break off so,
For we may pity, though not pardon thee.

Egeon. O, had the gods done so, I had not now
Worthily° termed them merciless to us.
100 For, ere the ships could meet by twice five leagues,
We were encount'red by a mighty rock,
Which being violently borne upon,
Our helpful ship° was splitted in the midst;
So that, in this unjust divorce of us,
105 Fortune had left to both of us alike
What to delight in, what to sorrow for.
Her part, poor soul, seeming as burdenèd
With lesser weight, but not with lesser woe,
Was carried with more speed before the wind;
110 And in our sight they three were taken up
By fishermen of Corinth, as we thought.
At length another ship had seized on us,
And, knowing whom it was their hap to save,
Gave healthful welcome to their shipwracked guests,
115 And would have reft° the fishers of their prey,
Had not their bark been very slow of sail;
And therefore homeward did they bend their course.

87 **Corinth** (major Greek seaport) 90 **his wishèd** its wished-for 92 **amain** with full speed 93 **Epidaurus** (ancient name for both a Greek and an Adriatic town) 99 **Worthily** deservedly 103 **ship** i.e., the mast 115 **reft** robbed

Thus have you heard me severed from my bliss,
That by misfortunes was my life prolonged
To tell sad stories of my own mishaps.   120

Duke. And, for the sake of them thou sorrowest for,
Do me the favor to dilate° at full
What have befall'n of them and thee till now.

Egeon. My youngest boy, and yet my eldest care,
At eighteen years became inquisitive   125
After his brother, and importuned me
That his attendant—so his case was like,
Reft of his brother, but retained his name—
Might bear him company in the quest of him;
Whom whilst I labored of a love° to see,   130
I hazarded the loss of whom I loved.
Five summers have I spent in farthest Greece,
Roaming clean through the bounds of Asia,
And coasting homeward, came to Ephesus,
Hopeless to find,° yet loath to leave unsought   135
Or° that or any place that harbors men.
But here must end the story of my life;
And happy were I in my timely death,
Could all my travels° warrant me they live.

Duke. Hapless Egeon, whom the fates have marked   140
To bear the extremity of dire mishap!
Now trust me, were it not against our laws,
Against my crown, my oath, my dignity,°
Which princes, would they, may not disannul,°
My soul should sue as advocate for thee.   145
But though thou art adjudgèd° to the death,
And passèd sentence may not be recalled
But to our honor's great disparagement,°
Yet will I favor thee in what I can;
Therefore, merchant, I'll limit thee this day   150
To seek thy health by beneficial help.
Try all the friends thou hast in Ephesus—

122 dilate relate   130 of a love out of love   135 Hopeless to find
without hope of finding   136 Or either   139 travels (with the further implication of "travails")   143 dignity office   144 disannul
cancel   146 adjudgèd sentenced   148 disparagement injury

Beg thou, or borrow, to make up the sum,
And live; if no, then thou art doomed to die.
155   Jailer, take him to thy custody.

Jailer. I will, my lord.

Egeon. Hopeless and helpless doth Egeon wend,
But to procrastinate° his lifeless end.   *Exeunt*

[Scene II. *The Mart.°*]

Enter Antipholus [of Syracuse], a Merchant, and
Dromio [of Syracuse].

Merchant. Therefore, give out you are of Epidamnum
Lest that your goods too soon be confiscate.
This very day a Syracusian merchant
Is apprehended for arrival here,
5   And not being able to buy out° his life,
According to the statute of the town,
Dies ere the weary sun set in the west.
There is your money that I had to keep.

S. Antipholus. Go bear it to the Centaur,° where we
host,°
10   And stay there, Dromio, till I come to thee;
Within this hour it will be dinnertime;
Till that, I'll view the manners of the town,
Peruse the traders, gaze upon the buildings,
And then return and sleep within mine inn;
15   For with long travel I am stiff and weary.
Get thee away.

S. Dromio. Many a man would take you at your word
And go indeed, having so good a mean.°
Exit Dromio

158 **procrastinate** postpone   I.ii.s.d. **Mart** marketplace   5 **buy out**
redeem   9 **Centaur** (name and sign of an inn)   9 **host** lodge   1
mean means

S. Antipholus. A trusty villain,° sir, that very oft,
When I am dull with care and melancholy, 20
Lightens my humor° with his merry jests.
What, will you walk with me about the town,
And then go to my inn and dine with me?

Merchant. I am invited, sir, to certain merchants,
Of whom I hope to make much benefit. 25
I crave your pardon; soon at five o'clock,
Please you, I'll meet with you upon the Mart,
And afterward consort° you till bedtime.
My present business calls me from you now.

S. Antipholus. Farewell till then. I will go lose myself, 30
And wander up and down to view the city.

Merchant. Sir, I commend you to your own content.
                                                        Exit.

S. Antipholus. He that commends me to mine own content
Commends me to the thing I cannot get.
I to the world am like a drop of water 35
That in the ocean seeks another drop,
Who, falling there to find his fellow forth,°
Unseen, inquisitive, confounds° himself.
So I, to find a mother and a brother,
In quest of them, unhappy,° lose myself. 40

Enter Dromio of Ephesus.

Here comes the almanac° of my true date.
What now? How chance thou art returned so soon?

E. Dromio. Returned so soon! Rather approached too
    late.
The capon burns, the pig falls from the spit;
The clock hath strucken twelve° upon the bell; 45
My mistress made it one upon my cheek.
She is so hot because the meat is cold;

19 **villain** (in the original sense of "bondman") 21 **humor** mood
28 **consort** accompany 37 **find his fellow forth** seek his fellow out
38 **confounds** loses 40 **unhappy** unlucky 41 **almanac** (Dromio
reminds Antipholus of his own age) 45 **twelve** (dinnertime or later)

The meat is cold because you come not home;
You come not home because you have no stomach;°
50 You have no stomach, having broke your fast.
But we, that know what 'tis to fast and pray,
Are penitent for your default° today.

S. Antipholus. Stop in your wind,° sir; tell me this
    I pray:
Where have you left the money that I gave you?

55 *E. Dromio.* O, sixpence, that I had o' Wednesday last
To pay the saddler for my mistress' crupper?°
The saddler had it, sir, I kept it not.

S. Antipholus. I am not in a sportive humor now.
Tell me, and dally not, where is the money?
60 We being strangers here, how dar'st thou trust
So great a charge from thine own custody?

E. Dromio. I pray you, jest, sir, as you sit at dinner.
I from my mistress come to you in post;°
If I return, I shall be post° indeed,
65 For she will score° your fault upon my pate.
Methinks your maw,° like mine, should be your
    clock,
And strike you home without a messenger.

S. Antipholus. Come, Dromio, come, these jests are
    out of season;
Reserve them till a merrier hour than this.
70 Where is the gold I gave in charge to thee?

E. Dromio. To me, sir? Why, you gave no gold to me.

S. Antipholus. Come on, sir knave, have done your
    foolishness,
And tell me how thou hast disposed thy charge.

49 **stomach** appetite   52 **default** (1) sin (2) failure to appear   5
wind breath   56 **crupper** strap from saddle to horse's tail   63 **pos**
haste   64 **post** posted (to pay account, with pun meaning "beaten"
65 **score** (with pun on "scour," beat)   66 **maw** stomach (ordinaril
used of animals)

E. Dromio. My charge was but to fetch you from the
    Mart
    Home to your house, the Phoenix,° sir, to dinner.   75
    My mistress and her sister stays for you.

S. Antipholus. Now, as I am a Christian, answer me,
    In what safe place you have bestowed° my money;
    Or I shall break that merry sconce° of yours
    That stands on° tricks when I am undisposed.   80
    Where is the thousand marks thou hadst of me?

E. Dromio. I have some marks of yours upon my pate,
    Some of my mistress' marks upon my shoulders,
    But not a thousand marks between you both.
    If I should pay° your worship those again,   85
    Perchance you will not bear them patiently.

S. Antipholus. Thy mistress' marks? What mistress,
    slave, hast thou?

E. Dromio. Your worship's wife, my mistress at the
    Phoenix;
    She that doth fast till you come home to dinner,
    And prays that you will hie you home to dinner.   90

S. Antipholus. What, wilt thou flout me thus unto my
    face,
    Being forbid? There, take you that, sir knave.
                             [Beats him.]

E. Dromio. What mean you, sir? For God's sake, hold
    your hands!
    Nay, and° you will not, sir, I'll take my heels.
                             Exit Dromio E.

S. Antipholus. Upon my life, by some device or other,   95
    The villain is o'er-raught° of all my money.
    They say this town is full of cozenage:°
    As° nimble jugglers that deceive the eye,

---

75 **Phoenix** i.e., house of Antipholus, denoted by the sign of his shop
78 **bestowed** deposited   79 **sconce** head   80 **stands on** insists upon
85 **pay** (also meaning "beat")   94 **and** if   96 **o'er-raught** over-
reached   97 **cozenage** cheating   98 **As** such as

Dark-working sorcerers that change the mind,
100 Soul-killing witches that deform the body,
Disguisèd cheaters, prating mountebanks,°
And many suchlike liberties° of sin.
If it prove so, I will be gone the sooner.
I'll to the Centaur, to go seek this slave.
105 I greatly fear my money is not safe.   *Exit.*

101 **mountebanks** quacks   102 **liberties** uninhibited acts

ACT II

[Scene I. *The Phoenix.*]

*Enter Adriana, wife to Antipholus [of Ephesus], with
Luciana, her sister.*

Adriana. Neither my husband nor the slave returned,
That in such haste I sent to seek his master.
Sure, Luciana, it is two o'clock.

Luciana. Perhaps some merchant hath invited him,
And from the Mart he's somewhere gone to dinner.   5
Good sister, let us dine, and never fret;
A man is master of his liberty.
Time is their master, and when they see time,
They'll go or come; if so, be patient, sister.

Adriana. Why should their liberty than ours be more?   10

Luciana. Because their business still° lies out o' door.

Adriana. Look when° I serve him so, he takes it ill.

Luciana. O, know he is the bridle of your will.

Adriana. There's none but asses will be bridled so.

Luciana. Why, headstrong liberty is lashed° with woe.   15
There's nothing situate under heaven's eye
But hath his bound, in earth, in sea, in sky.
The beasts, the fishes, and the wingèd fowls
Are their males' subjects, and at their controls;°

II.i.11 **still** always   12 **Look when** whenever   15 **lashed** whipped
19 **controls** commands

20 Man, more divine, the master of all these,
    Lord of the wide world and wild wat'ry seas,
    Indued with intellectual sense° and souls,
    Of more preeminence than fish and fowls,
    Are masters to their females, and their lords;
25 Then let your will attend on their accords.

Adriana. This servitude makes you to keep unwed.

Luciana. Not this, but troubles of the marriage bed.

Adriana. But, were you wedded, you would bear some
    sway.°

Luciana. Ere I learn love, I'll practice to obey.

Adriana. How if your husband start some other
30   where?°

Luciana. Till he come home again, I would forbear.

Adriana. Patience unmoved! no marvel though she
    pause;°
    They can be meek that have no other cause.°
    A wretched soul, bruised with adversity,
35 We bid be quiet when we hear it cry;
    But were we burd'ned with like weight of pain,
    As much or more we should ourselves complain:
    So thou, that hast no unkind mate to grieve thee,
    With urging helpless° patience would relieve me;
40 But, if thou live to see like right bereft,°
    This fool-begged° patience in thee will be left.

Luciana. Well, I will marry one day, but to try.
    Here comes your man, now is your husband nigh.

Enter Dromio of Ephesus.

Adriana. Say, is your tardy master now at hand?

---

22 **intellectual sense** reason   28 **sway** authority   30 **start some other where** pursue another woman   32 **pause** delay in getting married 33 **cause** motive   39 **helpless** unavailing   40 **like right bereft** your own rights denied 41 **fool-begged** i.e., assumed as one would assume responsibility for a fool

E. Dromio. Nay, he's at two hands with me, and that   45
   my two ears can witness.

Adriana. Say, didst thou speak with him? Know'st thou
   his mind?

E. Dromio. Ay, ay, he told° his mind upon mine ear.
   Beshrew his hand, I scarce could understand it.

Luciana. Spake he so doubtfully,° thou couldst not   50
   feel his meaning?

E. Dromio. Nay, he struck so plainly, I could too well
   feel his blows; and withal so doubtfully, that I could
   scarce understand° them.

Adriana. But say, I prithee, is he coming home?   55
   It seems he hath great care to please his wife.

E. Dromio. Why, mistress, sure my master is horn-mad.

Adriana. Horn-mad,° thou villain!

E. Dromio.   I mean not cuckold-mad,
   But sure he is stark mad.
   When I desired him to come home to dinner,   60
   He asked me for a thousand marks in gold.
   "'Tis dinnertime," quoth I. "My gold!" quoth he.
   "Your meat doth burn," quoth I. "My gold!" quoth
      he.
   "Will you come?" quoth I. "My gold!" quoth he.
   "Where is the thousand marks I gave thee, villain?"   65
   "The pig," quoth I, "is burned." "My gold!" quoth
      he.
   "My mistress, sir—" quoth I. "Hang up° thy mis-
      tress!
   I know not thy mistress, out on° thy mistress!"

Luciana. Quoth who?

E. Dromio. Quoth my master.   70
   "I know," quoth he, "no house, no wife, no mistress."

48 **told** (with a pun on "tolled")   50 **doubtfully** uncertainly   54 **understand** (pun on "stand under")   58 **Horn-mad** (1) like a mad bull (2) a cuckold   67 **Hang up** be hanged   68 **out on** (angry interjection)

So that my errand due unto° my tongue,
I thank him, I bare° home upon my shoulders;
· For, in conclusion, he did beat me there.

Adriana. Go back again, thou slave, and fetch him
75   home.

E. Dromio. Go back again, and be new beaten home?
For God's sake, send some other messenger.

Adriana. Back, slave, or I will break thy pate across.°

E. Dromio. And he will bless that cross with other
beating;
80   Between you, I shall have a holy° head.

Adriana. Hence, prating peasant! Fetch thy master
home.

E. Dromio. Am I so round° with you, as you with me,
That like a football you do spurn me thus?
You spurn me hence, and he will spurn me hither;
85   If I last in this service, you must case me in leather.
          [*Exit.*]

Luciana. Fie, how impatience lowereth° in your face!

Adriana. His company must do his minions° grace,
Whilst I at home starve° for a merry look:
Hath homely age th' alluring beauty took
90   From my poor cheek? Then he hath wasted it.
Are my discourses° dull? Barren my wit?
If voluble and sharp discourse be marred,
Unkindness blunts it more than marble hard.
Do their gay vestments his affections bait?°
95   That's not my fault; he's master of my state.
What ruins are in me that can be found,
By him not ruined? Then is he the ground
Of my defeatures.° My decayèd fair°

72 **due unto** appropriate to   73 **bare** bore   78 **across** (taken by
Dromio as "a cross")   80 **holy** (quibbling on "full of holes")   82
round (1) plain-spoken (2) spherical   86 **lowereth** frowns   87 **min-
ions** paramours   88 **starve** pine away   91 **discourses** conversations
94 **bait** entice   98 **defeatures** disfigurements   98 **decayèd fair** im-
paired beauty

A sunny look of his would soon repair.
But, too unruly deer,° he breaks the pale,°   *100*
And feeds from° home; poor I am but his stale.°

Luciana. Self-harming jealousy! fie, beat it hence.

Adriana. Unfeeling fools can with such wrongs dis-
    pense.°
I know his eye doth homage otherwhere,°
Or else what lets° it but he would be here?   *105*
Sister, you know he promised me a chain.
Would that alone, alone he would detain,°
So he would keep fair quarter° with his bed!
I see the jewel best enamelèd
Will lose his° beauty; yet the gold bides still   *110*
That others touch, and often touching will
Wear gold, and no man that hath a name
But falsehood and corruption doth it shame.°
Since that my beauty cannot please his eye,
I'll weep what's left away, and weeping die.   *115*

Luciana. How many fond° fools serve mad jealousy!
                    Exit [with Adriana].

[Scene II. *The Mart.*]

Enter Antipholus [of Syracuse].

S. Antipholus. The gold I gave to Dromio is laid up
    Safe at the Centaur, and the heedful slave
    Is wand'red forth, in care to seek me out,
    By computation° and mine host's report.

100 deer (pun on "dear")   100 pale enclosure   101 from away from
101 stale dupe   103 dispense offer a dispensation   104 otherwhere
elsewhere   105 lets prevents   107 detain keep back   108 keep fair
quarter keep the peace   110 his its   109–113 I see . . . it shame
(through these ambiguous metaphors Adriana seems to imply that
she still values her husband, though he is made less attractive by
promiscuity)   116 fond foolish   II.ii.4 computation calculation

5   I could not speak with Dromio since at first
I sent him from the Mart! See, here he comes.

Enter Dromio of Syracuse.

How now, sir, is your merry humor altered?
As you love strokes, so jest with me again.
You know no Centaur? You received no gold?
10   Your mistress sent to have me home to dinner?
My house was at the Phoenix? Wast thou mad,
That thus so madly thou didst answer me?

S. Dromio. What answer, sir? When spake I such a
word?

S. Antipholus. Even now, even here, not half an hour
since.

15   *S. Dromio.* I did not see you since you sent me hence,
Home to the Centaur, with the gold you gave me.

S. Antipholus. Villain, thou didst deny the gold's
receipt,
And told'st me of a mistress, and a dinner;
For which, I hope, thou felt'st I was displeased.

20   *S. Dromio.* I am glad to see you in this merry vein.
What means this jest? I pray you, master, tell me.

S. Antipholus. Yea, dost thou jeer, and flout me in the
teeth?°
Think'st thou, I jest? Hold, take thou that! And that!
Beats Dromio.

S. Dromio. Hold, sir, for God's sake! Now your jest is
earnest.°
25   Upon what bargain do you give it me?

S. Antipholus. Because that I familiarly sometimes
Do use you for my fool and chat with you,
Your sauciness will jest upon my love,
And make a common° of my serious hours.
30   When the sun shines, let foolish gnats make sport

22 **in the teeth** to my face   24 **earnest** (1) serious (2) a deposit
29 **common** public property

But creep in crannies, when he hides his beams.
If you will jest with me, know my aspect,°
And fashion your demeanor to my looks,
Or I will beat this method in your sconce.°

S. Dromio. Sconce, call you it? So you would leave   35
battering, I had rather have it a head. And you use
these blows long, I must get a sconce for my head,
and ensconce° it too, or else I shall seek my wit° in
my shoulders. But, I pray, sir, why am I beaten?

S. Antipholus. Dost thou not know?   40

S. Dromio. Nothing, sir, but that I am beaten.

S. Antipholus. Shall I tell you why?

S. Dromio. Ay, sir, and wherefore; for they say every
why hath a wherefore.

S. Antipholus. Why, first for flouting me, and then
wherefore,   45
For urging it the second time to me.

S. Dromio. Was there ever any man thus beaten out of
season,
When in the why and the wherefore is neither rhyme
nor reason?
Well, sir, I thank you.

S. Antipholus.   Thank me, sir, for what?

S. Dromio. Marry,° sir, for this something that you   50
gave me for nothing.

S. Antipholus. I'll make you amends next, to give you
nothing for something. But say, sir, is it dinnertime?

S. Dromio. No, sir. I think the meat wants that° I
have.   55

S. Antipholus. In good time,° sir. What's that?

32 aspect attitude (astrological term for planetary influence)   34
sconce (1) head (2) fortification   38 ensconce screen   38 wit brains
50 Marry (mild exclamation, originally an oath by the Virgin Mary)
54 wants that lacks what   56 In good time indeed

S. Dromio. Basting.°

S. Antipholus. Well, sir, then 'twill be dry.

S. Dromio. If it be, sir, I pray you eat none of it.

60 *S. Antipholus.* Your reason?

S. Dromio. Lest it make you choleric° and purchase me another dry° basting.

S. Antipholus. Well, sir, learn to jest in good time; there's a time for all things.

65 *S. Dromio.* I durst have denied that, before you were so choleric.

S. Antipholus. By what rule, sir?

S. Dromio. Marry, sir, by a rule as plain as the plain bald pate of Father Time himself.

70 *S. Antipholus.* Let's hear it.

S. Dromio. There's no time for a man to recover his hair that grows bald by nature.

S. Antipholus. May he not do it by fine and recovery?°

75 *S. Dromio.* Yes, to pay a fine for a periwig and recover the lost hair of another man.

S. Antipholus. Why is Time such a niggard of hair, being, as it is, so plentiful an excrement?°

S. Dromio. Because it is a blessing that he bestows on
80 beasts: and what he hath scanted men in hair, he hath given them in wit.

S. Antipholus. Why, but there's many a man hath more hair than wit.

57 **Basting** (1) moistening meat (2) thrashing   61 **choleric** irascible (from a surplus of choler, the humor of dryness)   62 **dry** bloodless   73–74 **fine and recovery** (legal form of conveyance, with a pun on "foin," the fur of a polecat)   78 **excrement** outgrowth

S. Dromio. Not a man of those but he hath the wit to
lose his hair.   85

S. Antipholus. Why, thou didst conclude hairy men
plain dealers without wit.

S. Dromio. The plainer dealer, the sooner lost; yet he
loseth it in a kind of jollity.°

S. Antipholus. For what reason?   90

S. Dromio. For two; and sound° ones too.

S. Antipholus. Nay, not sound, I pray you.

S. Dromio. Sure ones, then.

S. Antipholus. Nay, not sure, in a thing falsing.°

S. Dromio. Certain ones, then.   95

S. Antipholus. Name them.

S. Dromio. The one, to save the money that he spends
in tiring;° the other, that at dinner they should not
drop in his porridge.

S. Antipholus. You would all this time have proved   100
there is no time for all things.

S. Dromio. Marry, and did, sir: namely, e'en no time
to recover hair lost by nature.

S. Antipholus. But your reason was not substantial
why there is no time to recover.   105

S. Dromio. Thus I mend it: Time himself is bald, and
therefore, to the world's end, will have bald fol-
lowers.

S. Antipholus. I knew 'twould be a bald° conclusion.

Enter Adriana and Luciana.

But soft, who wafts° us yonder?   110

89 loseth it in a kind of jollity (as a consequence of venereal disease)
91 sound (1) cogent (2) healthy 94 falsing deceptive 98 tiring
hairdressing 109 bald (with a quibble on "trivial") 110 wafts
beckons

Adriana. Ay, ay, Antipholus, look strange° and
    frown;
    Some other mistress hath thy sweet aspects.
    I am not Adriana, nor thy wife.
    The time was once when thou unurged wouldst vow
115   That never words were music to thine ear,
    That never object pleasing in thine eye,
    That never touch well welcome to thy hand,
    That never meat sweet-savored in thy taste,
    Unless I spake or looked or touched or carved° to
    thee.
120   How comes it now, my husband, O how comes it,
    That thou art then estrangèd from thyself?
    Thyself I call it, being strange to me,
    That, undividable, incorporate,
    Am better than thy dear self's better part.°
125   Ah, do not tear away thyself from me;
    For know, my love, as easy mayst thou fall°
    A drop of water in the breaking gulf,
    And take unmingled thence that drop again
    Without addition or diminishing
130   As take from me thyself, and not me too.
    How dearly° would it touch thee to the quick,
    Shouldst thou but hear I were licentious,
    And that this body, consecrate to thee,
    By ruffian lust should be contaminate!
135   Wouldst thou not spit at me, and spurn at me,
    And hurl the name of husband in my face,
    And tear the stained skin off my harlot brow,
    And from my false hand cut the wedding ring,
    And break it with a deep-divorcing vow?
140   I know thou canst, and therefore see thou do it.
    I am possessed with an adulterate blot.
    My blood is mingled with the crime° of lust;
    For, if we two be one, and thou play false,
    I do digest the poison of thy flesh,
145   Being strumpeted by thy contagion.

111 **strange** distant   119 **carved** (a way of flirting at the dinner table)
124 **better part** soul   126 **fall** let fall   131 **dearly** grievously   142
crime sin

Keep then fair league and truce with thy true bed,°
I live distained,° thou undishonorèd.

S. Antipholus. Plead you to me, fair dame? I know
    you not.
In Ephesus I am but two hours old,
As strange unto your town as to your talk;   *150*
Who,° every word by all my wit being scanned,
Wants wit in all one word to understand.

Luciana. Fie, brother, how the world is changed with
    you.
When were you wont to use my sister thus?
She sent for you by Dromio home to dinner.   *155*

S. Antipholus. By Dromio?

S. Dromio. By me?

Adriana. By thee, and this thou didst return from
    him:
That he did buffet thee, and in his blows
Denied my house for his, me for his wife.   *160*

S. Antipholus. Did you converse, sir, with this gentle-
    woman?
What is the course and drift° of your compact?°

S. Dromio. I, sir? I never saw her till this time.

S. Antipholus. Villain, thou liest; for even her very
    words
Didst thou deliver to me on the Mart.   *165*

S. Dromio. I never spake with her in all my life.

S. Antipholus. How can she thus then call us by our
    names,
Unless it be by inspiration?

Adriana. How ill agrees it with your gravity
To counterfeit thus grossly° with your slave,   *170*

146 Keep then . . . true bed i.e., if you are faithful to your marriage
147 distained unstained   151 Who (refers to "I")   162 course and
drift general meaning   162 compact confederacy   170 grossly obviously

Abetting him to thwart me in my mood!
Be it my wrong you are from me exempt,°
But wrong not that wrong with a more contempt.°
Come, I will fasten on° this sleeve of thine:
173 Thou art an elm, my husband, I a vine,
Whose weakness, married to thy stronger state,
Makes me with thy strength to communicate.°
If aught possess thee° from me, it is dross,
Usurping ivy, briar, or idle° moss,
180 Who, all for want of pruning, with intrusion
Infect thy sap and live on thy confusion.°

S. Antipholus. [*Aside*] To me she speaks, she moves
  me for her theme;°
What, was I married to her in my dream?
Or sleep I now, and think I hear all this?
185 What error drives our eyes and ears amiss?
Until I know this sure uncertainty,
I'll entertain the offered fallacy.°

Luciana. Dromio, go bid the servants spread for
  dinner.

S. Dromio. O, for my beads!° I cross me for a sinner.
190 This is the fairy land. O spite of spites!
We talk with goblins, owls, and sprites;
If we obey them not, this will ensue:
They'll suck our breath, or pinch us black and blue.

Luciana. Why prat'st thou to thyself and answer'st
  not?
Dromio, thou drone, thou snail, thou slug, thou
195   sot.°

S. Dromio. I am transformèd, master, am not I?

S. Antipholus. I think thou art in mind, and so am I.

---

172 exempt cut off   173 But wrong . . . more contempt i.e., do not
compound it by adding insult to injury   174 fasten on cling to
177 communicate share   178 possess thee take you away   179 idle
worthless   181 confusion ruin   182 moves me for her theme ap-
peals to me as her subject   187 fallacy delusion   189 beads rosary
195 sot dolt

S. Dromio. Nay, master, both in mind and in my
    shape.

S. Antipholus. Thou hast thine own form.

S. Dromio.   No, I am an ape.°

Luciana. If thou art changed to aught, 'tis to an ass.   *200*

S. Dromio. 'Tis true, she rides° me and I long for
    grass.
    'Tis so, I am an ass; else it could never be
    But I should know her as well as she knows me.

Adriana. Come, come, no longer will I be a fool,
    To put the finger in the eye and weep,   *205*
    Whilst man and master laughs my woes to scorn.
    Come, sir, to dinner. Dromio, keep the gate.
    Husband, I'll dine above° with you today,
    And shrive° you of a thousand idle pranks.
    Sirrah,° if any ask you for your master,   *210*
    Say he dines forth,° and let no creature enter.
    Come, sister. Dromio, play the porter well.

S. Antipholus. [*Aside*] Am I in earth, in heaven, or in
    hell?
    Sleeping or waking, mad or well-advised?°
    Known unto these, and to myself disguised?   *215*
    I'll say as they say, and persever so,
    And in this mist at all adventures° go.

S. Dromio. Master, shall I be porter at the gate?

Adriana. Ay, and let none enter, lest I break your
    pate.

Luciana. Come, come, Antipholus, we dine too late.   *220*
                             [*Exeunt.*]

---

199 ape imitation (or fool)   **201 rides** teases   **208 above** upstairs
(represented by the upper stage)   **209 shrive** hear confession and
absolve   **210 Sirrah** (term used in addressing inferiors)   **211 forth**
out   **214 well-advised** of sound mind   **217 adventures** hazards

ACT III

Scene I. [*Before the Phoenix.*]

*Enter Antipholus of Ephesus, his man Dromio,
Angelo the Goldsmith, and Balthasar the Merchant.*

E. Antipholus. Good Signor° Angelo, you must ex-
    cuse us all;
  My wife is shrewish when I keep not hours.
  Say that I lingered with you at your shop
  To see the making of her carcanet,°
5   And that tomorrow you will bring it home.
  But here's a villain that would face me down°
  He met me on the Mart, and that I beat him,
  And charged him with a thousand marks in gold,
  And that I did deny° my wife and house.
10 Thou drunkard, thou, what didst thou mean by this?

E. Dromio. Say what you will, sir, but I know what
    I know—
  That you beat me at the Mart, I have your hand° to
    show;
  If the skin were parchment and the blows you gave
    were ink,
  Your own handwriting would tell you what I think.

E. Antipholus. I think thou art an ass.

III.i.1 **Signor** (the Italian title of respect is applied rather broadly by
Shakespeare) 4 **carcanet** jeweled necklace 6 **face me down** con-
tradict me by declaring 9 **deny** disown 12 **hand** (1) handwriting
(2) blows

E. Dromio.   Marry, so it doth appear   *15*
  By the wrongs I suffer and the blows I bear.
  I should kick, being kicked, and being at that pass,°
  You would keep from my heels and beware of an
    ass.

E. Antipholus. You're sad,° Signor Balthasar; pray
  God, our cheer°
  May answer° my good will and your good welcome
    here.   *20*

Balthasar. I hold your dainties cheap, sir, and your
  welcome dear.

E. Antipholus. O, Signor Balthasar, either at flesh or
  fish,
  A tableful of welcome makes scarce one dainty
    dish.

Balthasar. Good meat, sir, is common; that every
  churl° affords.

E. Antipholus. And welcome more common, for that's
  nothing but words.   *25*

Balthasar. Small cheer and great welcome makes a
  merry feast.

E. Antipholus. Ay, to a niggardly host and more spar-
  ing guest.
  But though my cates° be mean, take them in good
    part;
  Better cheer may you have, but not with better
    heart.
  But soft, my door is locked; go, bid them let us in.   *30*

E. Dromio. Maud, Bridget, Marian, Cicely, Gillian,
  Ginn!

S. Dromio. [*Within*] Mome, malt-horse, capon, cox-
  comb, idiot, patch!°

17 at that pass in that predicament   19 sad serious   19 cheer entertainment   20 answer accord with   24 churl peasant   28 cates dainties   32 Mome . . . patch blockhead, drudge, cuckold, fool, idiot,
jester

Either get thee from the door or sit down at the
 hatch.°
Dost thou conjure for wenches, that thou call'st for
 such store,°
When one is one too many? Go, get thee from the
35 door.

E. Dromio. What patch is made our porter? My
 master stays in the street.

S. Dromio. Let him walk from whence he came, lest
 he catch cold on's° feet.

E. Antipholus. Who talks within there? Ho, open the
 door!

S. Dromio. Right sir, I'll tell you when, and you'll tell
 me wherefore.

E. Antipholus. Wherefore? For my dinner; I have not
40 dined today.

S. Dromio. Nor today here you must not; come again
 when you may.

E. Antipholus. What art thou that keep'st me out
 from the house I owe?°

S. Dromio. The porter for this time, sir, and my name
 is Dromio.

E. Dromio. O villain, thou hast stol'n both mine office
 and my name.
The one ne'er got me credit, the other mickle°
45 blame.
If thou hadst been Dromio today in my place,
Thou wouldst have changed thy face for a name,
 or thy name for an ass.°

Enter Luce [above].

---

33 **hatch** lower part of a divided door   34 **store** abundance   37 **on's**
in his   42 **owe** own   45 **mickle** much   47 **Thou wouldst ... an ass**
you would have been confused with someone else, or been made a
fool of (?)

Luce. What a coil° is there, Dromio? Who are those
  at the gate?

E. Dromio. Let my master in, Luce.

Luce.   Faith, no, he comes too late.
  And so tell your master.

E. Dromio.   O Lord, I must laugh!   50
  Have at you with a proverb:° "Shall I set in my
  staff?"°

Luce. Have at you with another: that's "When? Can
  you tell?"°

S. Dromio. If thy name be called Luce—Luce, thou
  hast answered him well.

E. Antipholus. Do you hear, you minion?° You'll let
  us in, I trow?

Luce. I thought to have asked you.

S. Dromio.   And you said no.   55

E. Dromio. So, come help! Well struck! There was
  blow for blow.

E. Antipholus. Thou baggage, let me in.

Luce.   Can you tell for whose sake?

E. Dromio. Master, knock the door hard.

Luce.   Let him knock till it ache.

E. Antipholus. You'll cry for this, minion, if I beat the
  door down.

Luce. What needs all that, and a pair of stocks° in
  the town?   60

Enter Adriana [above].

___

48 **coil** turmoil   51 **proverb** (they bandy proverbial phrases)   51 **set
in my staff** move in   52 **When? Can you tell?** (a contemptuous re-
tort)   54 **minion** hussy   60 **stocks** device for the public confinement
of offenders

Adriana. Who is that at the door that keeps all this noise?

S. Dromio. By my troth, your town is troubled with unruly boys.°

E. Antipholus. Are you there, wife? You might have come before.

Adriana. Your wife, sir knave! Go, get you from the door.   [*Exit with Luce.*]

65 *E. Dromio.* If you went in pain, master, this knave would go sore.

Angelo. Here is neither cheer, sir, nor welcome; we would fain have either.

Balthasar. In debating which was best, we shall part° with neither.

E. Dromio. They stand at the door, master. Bid them welcome hither.

E. Antipholus. There is something in the wind, that we cannot get in.

70 *E. Dromio.* You would say so, master, if your garments were thin.
Your cake here is warm within; you stand here in the cold.
It would make a man mad as a buck° to be so bought and sold.°

E. Antipholus. Go, fetch me something. I'll break ope the gate.

S. Dromio. Break any breaking here, and I'll break your knave's pate.

75 *E. Dromio.* A man may break° a word with you, sir, and words are but wind;°

---

62 **boys** fellows   67 **part** depart   72 **buck** male deer (with an implication of "horn-mad")   72 **bought and sold** cheated   75 **break** exchange   75 **words are but wind** (a proverb, which Dromio vulgarly quibbles upon)

Ay, and break it in your face, so he break it not
  behind.

S. Dromio. It seems thou want'st breaking.° Out upon
  thee,° hind!°

E. Dromio. Here's too much "out upon thee." I pray
  thee, let me in.

S. Dromio. Ay, when fowls have no feathers, and fish
  have no fin.

E. Antipholus. Well, I'll break in. Go borrow me a
  crow.°   80

E. Dromio. A crow without feather? Master, mean
  you so?
  For a fish without a fin, there's a fowl without a
  feather.
  If a crow help us in, sirrah, we'll pluck a crow°
  together.

E. Antipholus. Go, get thee gone, fetch me an iron
  crow.

Balthasar. Have patience, sir, O, let it not be so!   85
  Herein you war against your reputation,
  And draw within the compass of suspect°
  Th' unviolated honor of your wife.
  Once this°—your long experience of her wisdom,
  Her sober virtue, years, and modesty,   90
  Plead on her part some cause to you unknown;
  And doubt not, sir, but she will well excuse°
  Why at this time the doors are made° against you.
  Be ruled by me, depart in patience,
  And let us to the Tiger° all to dinner.   95
  And, about evening, come yourself alone,
  To know the reason of this strange restraint.
  If by strong hand you offer° to break in,

---

77 **breaking** beating   77 **Out upon thee** (a mild curse)   77 **hind**
menial   80 **crow** crowbar   83 **pluck a crow** pick a bone   87 **suspect** suspicion   89 **Once this** in summary   92 **excuse** explain   93
made shut   95 **Tiger** (name and sign of an inn)   98 **offer** attempt

Now in the stirring passage° of the day,
100 A vulgar° comment will be made of it;
And that supposèd by the common rout°
Against your yet ungallèd estimation,°
That may with foul intrusion enter in
And dwell upon your grave when you are dead;
105 For slander lives upon succession,°
For ever housed where it gets possession.

E. *Antipholus.* You have prevailed. I will depart in
        quiet,
And, in despite of mirth,° mean to be merry.
I know a wench of excellent discourse,
110 Pretty and witty; wild and yet, too, gentle;
There will we dine: this woman that I mean,
My wife—but, I protest, without desert—
Hath oftentimes upbraided me withal.
To her will we to dinner. [*To Angelo*] Get you
        home,
115 And fetch the chain; by this,° I know, 'tis made;
Bring it, I pray you, to the Porpentine,°
For there's the house. That chain will I bestow—
Be it for nothing but to spite my wife—
Upon mine hostess there. Good sir, make haste.
120 Since mine own doors refuse to entertain me,
I'll knock elsewhere, to see if they'll disdain me.

Angelo. I'll meet you at that place some hour hence.

E. *Antipholus.* Do so. This jest shall cost me some
        expense.   *Exeunt.*

99 **stirring passage** busy traffic   100 **vulgar** public   101 **rout** multi-
tude   102 **ungallèd estimation** unblemished repute   105 **succession**
its consequences   108 **in despite of mirth** though disinclined to mer-
riment   115 **by this** by this time   116 **Porpentine** porcupine (name
of the Courtesan's house)

[Scene II. *Above.*]

Enter Luciana, with Antipholus of Syracuse.

Luciana. And may it be that you have quite forgot
  A husband's office? Shall, Antipholus, hate
  Even in the spring of love thy love-springs° rot?
  Shall love, in building, grow so ruinate?°
  If you did wed my sister for her wealth,   5
  Then for her wealth's sake use her with more kind-
     ness;
  Or, if you like elsewhere,° do it by stealth,
  Muffle your false love with some show of blindness.
  Let not my sister read it in your eye;
  Be not thy tongue thy own shame's orator;   10
  Look sweet, speak fair, become disloyalty;°
  Apparel vice like virtue's harbinger.
  Bear a fair presence, though your heart be tainted,
  Teach sin the carriage° of a holy saint,
  Be secret-false: what need she be acquainted?   15
  What simple thief brags of his own attaint?°
  'Tis double wrong to truant° with your bed
  And let her read it in thy looks at board.°
  Shame hath a bastard fame,° well managèd;
  Ill deeds is doubled with an evil word.   20
  Alas, poor women! Make us but believe,
  Being compact of credit,° that you love us;
  Though others have the arm, show us the sleeve:
  We in your motion° turn, and you may move us.
  Then, gentle brother, get you in again;   25

III.ii.3 **love-springs** young plants of love 4 **ruinate** ruinous 7 **like elsewhere** have some other love 11 **become disloyalty** make infidel-ity seem becoming 14 **carriage** bearing 16 **attaint** disgrace 17 **truant** play truant 18 **board** table 19 **bastard fame** illegitimate honor 22 **compact of credit** disposed to trust 24 **in your motion** by your moves

Comfort my sister, cheer her, call her wife;
'Tis holy sport, to be a little vain,°
When the sweet breath of flattery conquers strife.

S. Antipholus. Sweet mistress, what your name is else,
  I know not;
30   Nor by what wonder you do hit of° mine;
  Less in your knowledge and your grace you show°
    not
  Than our earth's wonder,° more than earth divine.
  Teach me, dear creature, how to think and speak:
  Lay open to my earthy-gross conceit,°
35   Smoth'red in errors, feeble, shallow, weak,
  The folded° meaning of your words' deceit.
  Against my soul's pure truth why labor you
  To make it wander in an unknown field?
  Are you a god? Would you create me new?
40   Transform me, then, and to your pow'r I'll yield.
  But if that I am I, then well I know
  Your weeping sister is no wife of mine,
  Nor to her bed no homage do I owe;
  Far more, far more, to you do I decline.°
45   O, train° me not, sweet mermaid, with thy note,
  To drown me in thy sister's flood of tears.
  Sing, siren, for thyself, and I will dote;
  Spread o'er the silver waves thy golden hairs;
  And as a bed I'll take them, and there lie,
50   And, in that glorious supposition, think
  He gains by death that hath such means to die.°
  Let Love, being light,° be drownèd if she sink!

Luciana. What, are you mad, that you do reason so?

S. Antipholus. Not mad, but mated°—how, I do not
  know.

55 *Luciana.* It is a fault that springeth from your eye.

27 **be a little vain** use a little flattery   30 **hit of** hit on   31 **show** appear   32 **earth's wonder** (these lines are sometimes taken as a compliment to Queen Elizabeth)   34 **conceit** apprehension   36 **folded** hidden   44 **decline** incline   45 **train** lure   51 **die** (with an implication of sexual fulfillment)   52 **light** (1) not heavy (2) wanton   54 **mated** (1) confounded (2) wedded

S. Antipholus. For gazing on your beams, fair sun,
  being by.

Luciana. Gaze where you should, and that will clear
  your sight.

S. Antipholus. As good to wink,° sweet love, as look
  on night.

Luciana. Why call you me love? Call my sister so.

S. Antipholus. Thy sister's sister.

Luciana.   That's my sister.

S. Antipholus.   No,   60
  It is thyself, mine own self's better part,
  Mine eye's clear eye, my dear heart's dearer heart;
  My food, my fortune, and my sweet hope's aim;
  My sole earth's heaven, and my heaven's claim.°

Luciana. All this my sister is, or else should be.   65

S. Antipholus. Call thyself sister, sweet, for I am thee;
  Thee will I love, and with thee lead my life;
  Thou hast no husband yet, nor I no wife.
  Give me thy hand.

Luciana.   O, soft, sir, hold you still
  I'll fetch my sister, to get her good will.   *Exit.*   70

                Enter Dromio of Syracuse.

S. Antipholus. Why, how now, Dromio! Where run'st
  thou so fast?

S. Dromio. Do you know me, sir? Am I Dromio? Am
  I your man? Am I myself?

S. Antipholus. Thou art Dromio, thou art my man,   75
  thou art thyself.

S. Dromio. I am an ass; I am a woman's man, and
  besides myself.

---

58 **wink** shut one's eyes   64 **heaven's claim** claim on heaven

S. Antipholus. What woman's man? And how besides
80   thyself?

S. Dromio. Marry, sir, besides myself,° I am due° to
a woman: one that claims me, one that haunts me,
one that will have me.

S. Antipholus. What claim lays she to thee?

85   *S. Dromio.* Marry, sir, such claim as you would lay
to your horse; and she would have me as a beast°—
not that, I being a beast, she would have me, but
that she, being a very beastly creature, lays claim
to me.

90   *S. Antipholus.* What is she?

S. Dromio. A very reverend body; ay, such a one as
a man may not speak of without he say "sir-reverence."° I have but lean luck in the match, and
yet is she a wondrous fat marriage.

95   *S. Antipholus.* How dost thou mean a fat marriage?

S. Dromio. Marry, sir, she's the kitchen-wench, and
all grease;° and I know not what use to put her to,
but to make a lamp of her, and run from her by
her own light. I warrant her rags and the tallow in
100   them will burn a Poland winter. If she lives till
doomsday, she'll burn a week° longer than the
whole world.

S. Antipholus. What complexion is she of?

S. Dromio. Swart,° like my shoe, but her face noth-
105   ing like so clean kept; for why? She sweats; a man
may go over-shoes° in the grime of it.

S. Antipholus. That's a fault that water will mend.

---

81 besides myself (1) out of my mind (2) in addition to me   81 due
belonging   86 a beast (Elizabethan pronunciation made possible a
pun on "abased")   92–93 sir-reverence save your reverence (meaning "pardon the expression")   97 grease (with a pun on "grace")
101 week (with a pun on "wick")   104 Swart swarthy   106 over-
shoes shoe-deep

S. Dromio. No, sir, 'tis in grain;° Noah's flood could
not do it.

S. Antipholus. What's her name?　　　　　　　*110*

S. Dromio. Nell,° sir; but her name and three quarters—that's an ell° and three quarters—will not
measure her from hip to hip.

S. Antipholus. Then she bears some breadth?

S. Dromio. No longer from head to foot than from　*115*
hip to hip. She is spherical, like a globe. I could
find out countries in her.

S. Antipholus. In what part of her body stands Ire-
land?

S. Dromio. Marry, sir, in her buttocks; I found it out　*120*
by the bogs.

S. Antipholus. Where Scotland?

S. Dromio. I found it by the barrenness, hard in the
palm of the hand.

S. Antipholus. Where France?　　　　　　　*125*

S. Dromio. In her forehead, armed and reverted,°
making war against her heir.°

S. Antipholus. Where England?

S. Dromio. I looked for the chalky cliffs,° but I could
find no whiteness in them. But I guess, it stood in　*130*
her chin, by the salt rheum° that ran between
France and it.

S. Antipholus. Where Spain?

S. Dromio. Faith, I saw it not; but I felt it hot in her
breath.　　　　　　　　　　　　　　*135*

S. Antipholus. Where America, the Indies?

108 **in grain** inherent　111 **Nell** (called Luce, III.i.49)　112 **ell** forty-
five inches　126 **reverted** revolted　127 **heir** (interpreted as a contemporary allusion to the struggle of the Catholic League against
Henry of Navarre, who succeeded to the throne of France in 1593)
129 **chalky cliffs** teeth　131 **rheum** moisture from the nose

S. Dromio. O, sir, upon her nose, all o'er embellished
with rubies, carbuncles, sapphires, declining° their
rich aspect to the hot breath of Spain, who sent
140 whole armadoes of carracks° to be ballast° at her
nose.

S. Antipholus. Where stood Belgia, the Netherlands?°

S. Dromio. O, sir, I did not look so low. To conclude, this drudge, or diviner,° laid claim to me,
145 called me Dromio, swore I was assured° to her,
told me what privy marks I had about me, as the
mark of my shoulder, the mole in my neck, the
great wart on my left arm, that I, amazed, ran from
her as a witch.
And, I think, if my breast had not been made of
150   faith, and my heart of steel,
She had transformed me to a curtal dog,° and made
me turn i' th' wheel.°

S. Antipholus. Go, hie thee presently,° post to the
road,°
And if° the wind blow any way from shore,
I will not harbor° in this town tonight.
155 If any bark put forth, come to the Mart,
Where I will walk till thou return to me.
If everyone knows us, and we know none,
'Tis time, I think, to trudge, pack, and begone.°

S. Dromio. As from a bear a man would run for life,
160 So fly I from her that would be my wife.   *Exit.*

S. Antipholus. There's none but witches do inhabit
here,
And therefore 'tis high time that I were hence.
She that doth call me husband, even my soul
Doth for a wife abhor. But her fair sister,

138 declining inclining   140 armadoes of carracks fleets of galleons
(with possible reference to the Spanish Armada of 1588)   140 ballast
loaded   142 Belgia, the Netherlands the Low Countries   144 diviner witch   145 assured betrothed   151 curtal dog dog with
docked tail   151 wheel spit   152 presently immediately   152 road
harbor   153 And if if   154 harbor lodge   158 trudge, pack, and
begone (synonyms)

Possessed with such a gentle sovereign grace,   *165*
Of such enchanting presence and discourse,
Hath almost made me traitor to myself.
But, lest myself be guilty to° self-wrong,
I'll stop mine ears against the mermaid's song.

Enter Angelo with the chain.

Angelo. Master Antipholus—

S. Antipholus.   Ay, that's my name.   *170*

Angelo. I know it well, sir. Lo, here is the chain.
I thought to have ta'en you at the Porpentine.
The chain unfinished made me stay thus long.

S. Antipholus. What is your will that I shall do with
this?

Angelo. What please yourself, sir; I have made it for
you.   *175*

S. Antipholus. Made it for me, sir? I bespoke° it not.

Angelo. Not once, nor twice, but twenty times you
have.
Go home with it and please your wife withal,
And soon at suppertime I'll visit you,
And then receive my money for the chain.   *180*

S. Antipholus. I pray you, sir, receive the money now,
For fear you ne'er see chain nor money more.

Angelo. You are a merry man, sir. Fare you well.
Exit.

S. Antipholus. What I should think of this, I cannot
tell:
But this I think, there's no man is so vain°   *185*
That would refuse so fair an offered chain.
I see a man here needs not live by shifts,°
When in the streets he meets such golden gifts.
I'll to the Mart, and there for Dromio stay;
If any ship put out, then straight° away.   *Exit.*   *190*

168 **to** of   176 **bespoke** ordered   185 **vain** silly   187 **shifts** tricks
190 **straight** without delay

ACT IV

Scene I. [*The Mart.*]

*Enter a Merchant, [Angelo the] Goldsmith, and
an Officer.*

Merchant. You know since Pentecost° the sum is due
And since I have not much importuned you,
Nor now I had not, but that I am bound
To Persia, and want guilders for my voyage;
5   Therefore make present° satisfaction,
Or I'll attach° you by this officer.

Angelo. Even just the sum that I do owe to you
Is growing° to me by Antipholus,
And in the instant that I met with you
10   He had of me a chain. At five o'clock
I shall receive the money for the same.
Pleaseth° you, walk with me down to his house;
I will discharge my bond, and thank you too.

*Enter Antipholus of Ephesus, [and] Dromio
[of Ephesus] from the Courtesan's.*

Officer. That labor may you save. See where he
comes.

E. Antipholus. While I go to the goldsmith's house,
15   go thou

IV.i.1 **Pentecost** the fiftieth day after Easter   **5 present** immediate
6 attach arrest   **8 growing** accruing   **12 Pleaseth** may it please

And buy a rope's end;° that will I bestow
Among my wife and her confederates,
For locking me out of my doors by day.
But soft, I see the goldsmith; get thee gone,
Buy thou a rope, and bring it home to me.   20

E. Dromio. I buy a thousand pound a year! I buy a
    rope!°   *Exit Dromio.*

E. Antipholus. A man is well holp° up that trusts to
    you!
I promisèd your presence and the chain,
But neither chain nor goldsmith came to me.
Belike you thought our love would last too long,   25
If it were chained together, and therefore came not.

Angelo. Saving your merry humor, here's the note
How much your chain weighs to the utmost carat,
The fineness of the gold and chargeful° fashion—
Which doth amount to three odd ducats° more   30
Than I stand debted to this gentleman.
I pray you, see him presently° discharged,
For he is bound to sea, and stays but for it.

E. Antipholus. I am not furnished with the present
    money.
Besides, I have some business in the town.   35
Good signor, take the stranger to my house,
And with you take the chain, and bid my wife
Disburse the sum on the receipt thereof.
Perchance I will be there as soon as you.

Angelo. Then you will bring the chain to her your-
    self?   40

E. Antipholus. No, bear it with you, lest I come not
    time enough.°

---

16 **rope's end** (for flogging)   21 **I buy . . . a rope!** (Dromio's obscure irony seems motivated by his awareness that the rope's end
could be used on him)   22 **holp** helped   29 **chargeful** costly   30
ducats gold coins of varying origin and value   32 **presently** instantly
41 **time enough** in time

Angelo. Well, sir, I will. Have you the chain abou
you?

E. Antipholus. And if I have not, sir, I hope yo
have,
Or else you may return without your money.

45 *Angelo.* Nay, come, I pray you, sir, give me the chain
Both wind and tide stays for this gentleman,
And I, to blame,° have held him here too long.

E. Antipholus. Good Lord, you use this dalliance°
to excuse
Your breach of promise to the Porpentine.
50 I should have chid you for not bringing it,
But, like a shrew,° you first begin to brawl.

Merchant. The hour steals on; I pray you, sir, dispatch.

Angelo. You hear how he importunes me—the chain!

E. Antipholus. Why, give it to my wife, and fetch
your money.

Angelo. Come, come, you know, I gave it you even
55 now;
Either send the chain or send me by some token.

E. Antipholus. Fie, now you run this humor out of
breath.
Come, where's the chain? I pray you, let me see it.

Merchant. My business cannot brook this dalliance.
60 Good sir, say whe'er° you'll answer° me or no:
If not, I'll leave him to the officer.

E. Antipholus. I answer you! What should I answer
you?

Angelo. The money that you owe me for the chain.

E. Antipholus. I owe you none till I receive the chain.

65 *Angelo.* You know I gave it you half an hour since.

47 **to blame** blameworthy   48 **dalliance** tarrying   51 **shrew** scold
(male or female)   60 **whe'er** whether   60 **answer** pay

E. Antipholus. You gave me none; you wrong me
  much to say so.

Angelo. You wrong me more, sir, in denying it.
  Consider how it stands upon° my credit.

Merchant. Well, officer, arrest him at my suit.

Officer. I do,   *70*
  And charge you in the Duke's name to obey me.

Angelo. This touches me in reputation.
  Either consent to pay this sum for me,
  Or I attach you by this officer.

E. Antipholus. Consent to pay thee that I never had! *75*
  Arrest me, foolish fellow, if thou dar'st.

Angelo. Here is thy fee; arrest him, officer.
  I would not spare my brother in this case,
  If he should scorn me so apparently.°

Officer. I do arrest you, sir; you hear the suit.   *80*

E. Antipholus. I do obey thee, till I give thee bail.
  But, sirrah, you shall buy this sport as dear
  As all the metal in your shop will answer.

Angelo. Sir, sir, I shall have law in Ephesus,
  To your notorious shame, I doubt it not.   *85*

      Enter Dromio of Syracuse from the Bay.

S. Dromio. Master, there's a bark of Epidamnum,
  That stays but till her owner comes aboard,
  And then she bears away. Our fraughtage,° sir,
  I have conveyed aboard, and I have bought
  The oil, the balsamum,° and aqua-vitae.°   *90*
  The ship is in her trim,° the merry wind
  Blows fair from land; they stay for nought at all
  But for their owner, master,° and yourself.

---

68 **stands upon** concerns   79 **apparently** openly   88 **fraughtage**
cargo   90 **balsamum** balm   90 **aqua-vitae** brandy   91 **in her trim**
ready to sail   93 **master** captain (?)

E. Antipholus. How now! a madman? Why, thou
    peevish° sheep,°
95 What ship of Epidamnum stays for me?

S. Dromio. A ship you sent me to, to hire waftage.°

E. Antipholus. Thou drunken slave, I sent thee for a
    rope,
And told thee to what purpose and what end.

S. Dromio. You sent me for a rope's end° as soon.
100 You sent me to the bay, sir, for a bark.

E. Antipholus. I will debate this matter at more
    leisure,
And teach your ears to list° me with more heed.
To Adriana, villain, hie thee straight;
Give her this key, and tell her, in the desk
105 That's covered o'er with Turkish tapestry
There is a purse of ducats; let her send it.
Tell her I am arrested in the street,
And that shall bail me. Hie thee, slave, begone.
On, officer, to prison till it come.
                Exeunt [all but Dromio].

110 *S. Dromio.* To Adriana—that is where we dined,
Where Dowsabel° did claim me for her husband.
She is too big, I hope, for me to compass.°
Thither I must, although against my will;
For servants must their masters' minds fulfill.
                        Exit.

94 **peevish** silly   94 **sheep** (with a pun on "ship")   96 **waftage** passage by sea   99 **rope's end** (in the sense of "halter" here)   102 **list** listen to   111 **Dowsabel** (from *douce et belle*, sweet and pretty, an elaborate name for a heroine, ironically applied to Nell)   112 **compass** (1) obtain (2) embrace

[Scene II. *Before the Phoenix.*]

Enter Adriana and Luciana.

Adriana. Ah, Luciana, did he tempt thee so?
  Mightst thou perceive austerely° in his eye,
  That he did plead in earnest, yea or no?
  Looked he or red or pale, or sad or merrily?
  What observation mad'st thou in this case   *5*
  Of his heart's meteors tilting° in his face?

Luciana. First, he denied you had in him no right.°

Adriana. He meant he did me none; the more my
  spite.°

Luciana. Then swore he that he was a stranger here.

Adriana. And true he swore, though yet forsworn he
  were.   *10*

Luciana. Then pleaded I for you.

Adriana.   And what said he?

Luciana. That love I begged for you he begged of me.

Adriana. With what persuasion did he tempt thy love?

Luciana. With words that in an honest° suit might
  move.
  First he did praise my beauty, then my speech.   *15*

Adriana. Didst speak him fair?°

Luciana.   Have patience, I beseech.

IV.ii.2 **austerely** by the austerity   6 **heart's meteors tilting** emotions tossing   7 **denied . . . no right** (double negative)   8 **spite** vexation 14 **honest** honorable   16 **speak him fair** speak to him kindly

Adriana. I cannot, nor I will not, hold me still.
My tongue, though not my heart, shall have his°
    will.
He is deformèd, crookèd, old and sere,
20   Ill-faced, worse bodied, shapeless° everywhere:
Vicious, ungentle, foolish, blunt, unkind,
Stigmatical in making,° worse in mind.

Luciana. Who would be jealous then of such a one?
No evil lost is wailed when it is gone.

25   *Adriana.* Ah, but I think him better than I say;
And yet would herein others' eyes were worse.
Far from her nest the lapwing° cries away;
My heart prays for him, though my tongue do
    curse.

Enter Dromio of Syracuse.

S. Dromio. Here, go—the desk, the purse! Sweet
    now, make haste.

Luciana. How hast thou lost thy breath?

30   *S. Dromio.*   By running fast.

Adriana. Where is thy master, Dromio? Is he well?

S. Dromio. No, he's in Tartar limbo,° worse than
    hell:
A devil in an everlasting garment° hath him;
One whose hard heart is buttoned up with steel:
35   A fiend, a fairy,° pitiless and rough:
A wolf, nay worse, a fellow all in buff:°
A back-friend,° a shoulder-clapper,° one that coun-
    termands°
The passages of alleys, creeks,° and narrow lands

18 his its   20 shapeless unshapely   22 Stigmatical in making deformed in appearance   27 lapwing peewit (who draws intruders
away from its nest in the manner described)   32 Tartar limbo prison
as well as the outskirts of hell (the pagan Tartarus)   33 everlasting
garment leather coat, the police uniform   35 fairy malignant spirit
36 buff ox-hide   37 back-friend false friend (with a quibble on the
mode of arrest)   37 shoulder-clapper bailiff   37 countermands pro-
hibits   38 creeks winding alleys

A hound that runs counter,° and yet draws dry-
   foot° well;
One that, before the judgment, carries poor souls
   to hell.   *40*

Adriana. Why, man, what is the matter?

S. Dromio. I do not know the matter, he is 'rested°
   on the case.°

Adriana. What, is he arrested? Tell me, at whose suit.

S. Dromio. I know not at whose suit he is arrested
   well;
But is in a suit of buff which 'rested him, that can
   I tell.   *45*
Will you send him, Mistress Redemption, the
   money in his desk?

Adriana. Go fetch it, sister. This I wonder at,
                               Exit Luciana.
Thus he, unknown to me, should be in debt.
Tell me, was he arrested on a band?°

S. Dromio. Not on a band, but on a stronger thing: *50*
A chain, a chain! Do you not hear it ring?

Adriana. What, the chain?

S. Dromio.   No, no, the bell; 'tis time
   that I were gone.
It was two ere I left him, and now the clock strikes
   one.°

Adriana. The hours come back! That did I never
   hear.

S. Dromio. O yes. If any hour° meet a sergeant, 'a°
   turns back for very fear.   *55*

---

39 **counter** (1) contrary (2) Counter, a debtors' prison 39 **draws
dry-foot** hunts by scent 42 **'rested** arrested 42 **case** (1) special
case at law (2) suit of clothes 49 **band** bond 53 **one** (with a pun
on "on") 55 **hour** (pun on "whore") 55 **'a** (colloquial form of
"he," "she," or "it")

Adriana. As if time were in debt! How fondly° dost
thou reason!

S. Dromio. Time is a very bankrupt, and owes more
than he's worth to season.°
Nay, he's a thief too: have you not heard men say,
That time comes stealing on by night and day?
60   If 'a be in debt and theft, and a sergeant in the way,
Hath he not reason to turn back an hour in a day?

Enter Luciana.

Adriana. Go, Dromio. There's the money, bear it
straight,
And bring thy master home immediately.
Come, sister. I am pressed down with conceit:°
65   Conceit, my comfort and my injury.
                    Exit [with Luciana and Dromio].

[Scene III. *The Mart.*]

Enter Antipholus of Syracuse.

S. Antipholus. There's not a man I meet but doth
salute me
As if I were their well-acquainted friend;
And everyone doth call me by my name.
Some tender money to me, some invite me;
5   Some other° give me thanks for kindnesses;
Some offer me commodities to buy.
Even now a tailor called me in his shop
And showed me silks that he had bought for me,
And therewithal took measure of my body.
10   Sure, these are but imaginary wiles,°
And Lapland° sorcerers inhabit here.

56 **fondly** foolishly   57 **season** occasion(?), ripen(?)   64 **conceit** imagination   IV.iii.5 **other** others   10 **imaginary wiles** tricks of the
imagination   11 **Lapland** (notorious for sorcery)

Enter Dromio of Syracuse.

S. Dromio. Master, here's the gold you sent me for.
What, have you got the picture of old Adam° new-
appareled?

S. Antipholus. What gold is this? What Adam dost   *15*
thou mean?

S. Dromio. Not that Adam that kept the paradise, but
that Adam that keeps the prison; he that goes in the
calf's skin° that was killed for the Prodigal; he that
came behind you, sir, like an evil angel, and bid   *20*
you forsake your liberty.

S. Antipholus. I understand thee not.

S. Dromio. No? Why, 'tis a plain case:° he that went,
like a bass-viol, in a case of leather; the man, sir,
that, when gentlemen are tired gives them a sob°   *25*
and 'rests them; he, sir, that takes pity on decayed
men, and gives them suits of durance;° he that sets
up his rest° to do more exploits with his mace°
than a morris-pike.°

S. Antipholus. What, thou mean'st an officer?   *30*

S. Dromio. Ay, sir, the sergeant of the band: he that
brings any man to answer it that breaks his band;°
one that thinks a man always going to bed, and
says, "God give you good rest!"°

S. Antipholus. Well, sir, there rest in your foolery.   *35*
Is there any ships puts forth tonight? May we be
gone?

S. Dromio. Why, sir, I brought you word an hour

---

13 old Adam the sergeant in his buff coat (?)   18–19 goes in the
calf's skin wears the leather garb (with a quibble on the fatted
calf in the parable)   23 case (1) situation (2) box (3) suit   25 sob
rest given a horse to recover its wind (with quibbles)   27 suits
of durance durable clothing (with puns on "lawsuits" and "imprisonment")   27–28 sets up his rest stakes all   28 mace staff of authority   29 morris-pike Moorish lance   32 band (with pun on "bond")
34 rest (with the usual pun)

since that the bark° *Expedition* put forth tonight,
40 and then were you hind'red by the sergeant to tarry
for the hoy° *Delay*. Here are the angels° that you
sent for to deliver you.

S. Antipholus. The fellow is distract, and so am I,
And here we wander in illusions.
45 Some blessèd power deliver us from hence!

Enter a Courtesan.

Courtesan. Well met, well met, Master Antipholus.
I see, sir, you have found the goldsmith now.
Is that the chain you promised me today?

S. Antipholus. Satan, avoid!° I charge thee, tempt me
not!

50 *S. Dromio.* Master, is this Mistress Satan?

S. Antipholus. It is the devil.

S. Dromio. Nay, she is worse, she is the devil's dam;°
and here she comes in the habit° of a light° wench,
and thereof comes that the wenches say, "God
55 damn me." That's as much to say, "God make me
a light wench." It is written, they appear to men
like angels of light. Light is an effect of fire, and
fire will burn: ergo,° light wenches will burn.°
Come not near her.

Courtesan. Your man and you are marvelous merry,
60 sir.
Will you go with me? We'll mend° our dinner here.

S. Dromio. Master, if you do, expect spoon-meat,° or
bespeak a long spoon.

S. Antipholus. Why, Dromio?

---

39 **bark** ship (allegorically named by Dromio)   41 **hoy** coasting vessel   41 **angels** coins worth ten shillings (with pun)   49 **avoid** begone (Matthew 4:10)   52 **dam** mother   53 **habit** dress   53 **light** (with implication of loose morals)   58 **ergo** it follows logically   58 **burn** infect with disease   61 **mend** complete   62 **spoon-meat** soft food (introducing an allusion to the proverb about the devil)

S. Dromio. Marry, he must have a long spoon that *65*
  must eat with the devil.

S. Antipholus. Avoid, then, fiend! What tell'st thou
  me of supping?
  Thou art, as you are all, a sorceress.
  I conjure° thee to leave me and be gone.

Courtesan. Give me the ring of mine you had at
  dinner,   *70*
  Or, for my diamond, the chain you promised,
  And I'll be gone, sir, and not trouble you.

S. Dromio. Some devils ask but the parings° of one's
  nail,
  A rush, a hair, a drop of blood, a pin,
  A nut, a cherry-stone;   *75*
  But she, more covetous, would have a chain.
  Master, be wise; and if you give it her,
  The devil will shake her chain, and fright us with it.

Courtesan. I pray you, sir, my ring, or else the chain.°
  I hope you do not mean to cheat me so!   *80*

S. Antipholus. Avaunt,° thou witch! Come, Dromio,
  let us go.

S. Dromio. Fly pride, says the peacock.° Mistress,
  that you know.   *Exit [with Antipholus].*

Courtesan. Now, out of doubt, Antipholus is mad,
  Else would he never so demean° himself.
  A ring he hath of mine worth forty ducats,   *85*
  And for the same he promised me a chain;
  Both one and other he denies me now.
  The reason that I gather he is mad,
  Besides this present instance of his rage,°
  Is a mad tale he told today at dinner,   *90*
  Of his own doors being shut against his entrance.
  Belike his wife, acquainted with his fits,

---

69 conjure solemnly call on   **73 parings** (witchcraft requires such
appurtenances in order to cast a spell)   **79 chain** (cf. Revelation,
20:1–2)   **81 Avaunt** away   **82 peacock** (emblem of pride, which was
also personified by a harlot)   **84 demean** behave   **89 rage** madness

On purpose shut the doors against his way.
My way is now to hie home to his house,
95   And tell his wife that, being lunatic,
He rushed into my house and took perforce°
My ring away. This course I fittest choose,
For forty ducats is too much to lose.   [*Exit.*]

[Scene IV. *The same.*]

Enter Antipholus of Ephesus with a Jailer.

E. Antipholus. Fear me not, man, I will not break
away.
I'll give thee, ere I leave thee, so much money,
To warrant° thee, as I am 'rested for.
My wife is in a wayward mood today,
5   And will not lightly trust the messenger
That I should be attached° in Ephesus;
I tell you, 'twill sound harshly in her ears.

Enter Dromio of Ephesus, with a rope's end.

Here comes my man, I think he brings the money.
How now, sir! Have you that I sent you for?

E. Dromio. Here's that, I warrant you, will pay° them
10   all.

E. Antipholus. But where's the money?

E. Dromio. Why, sir, I gave the money for the rope.

E. Antipholus. Five hundred ducats, villain, for a
rope?

E. Dromio. I'll serve you,° sir, five hundred at the
rate.

96 **perforce** by force   IV.iv.3 **warrant** secure   6 **attached** arrested
10 **pay** (with a beating)   14 **serve you** supply you with

E. Antipholus. To what end° did I bid thee hie thee
   home?   15

E. Dromio. To a rope's end, sir, and to that end am
   I returned.

E. Antipholus. And to that end, sir, I will welcome
   you.   [*Beats Dromio.*]

Officer. Good sir, be patient.

E. Dromio. Nay, 'tis for me to be patient; I am in
   adversity.   20

Officer. Good° now, hold thy tongue.

E. Dromio. Nay, rather persuade him to hold his
   hands.

E. Antipholus. Thou whoreson,° senseless villain!

E. Dromio. I would I were senseless, sir, that I might   25
   not feel your blows.

E. Antipholus. Thou art sensible° in nothing but
   blows, and so is an ass.

E. Dromio. I am an ass, indeed; you may prove it by
   my long ears.° I have served him from the hour of   30
   my nativity to this instant, and have nothing at his
   hands for my service but blows. When I am cold,
   he heats me with beating; when I am warm, he
   cools me with beating. I am waked with it when
   I sleep, raised with it when I sit, driven out of   35
   doors with it when I go from home, welcomed
   home with it when I return; nay, I bear it on my
   shoulders, as a beggar wont° her brat; and, I think,
   when he hath lamed me, I shall beg with it from
   door to door.   40

   Enter Adriana, Luciana, Courtesan, and a
        Schoolmaster called Pinch.

---

15 **end** purpose (on which Dromio quibbles)   21 **Good** (used voca-
tively)   24 **whoreson** bastard   27 **sensible** (1) reasonable (2) sensitive   30 **ears** (pun on "years")   38 **wont** habitually does

E. Antipholus. Come, go along; my wife is coming
yonder.

E. Dromio. Mistress, *"respice finem,"*° respect your
end; or rather, the prophecy like the parrot,° "beware the rope's end."

45 *E. Antipholus.* Wilt thou still talk?   *Beats Dromio.*

Courtesan. How say you now? Is not your husband
mad?

Adriana. His incivility confirms no less.
Good Doctor Pinch, you are a conjurer;°
Establish him in his true sense again,
50 And I will please° you what you will demand.

Luciana. Alas, how fiery and how sharp he looks!

Courtesan. Mark how he trembles in his ecstasy!°

Pinch. Give me your hand, and let me feel your pulse.
                              [*Antipholus strikes him.*]

E. Antipholus. There is my hand, and let it feel your
ear!

55 *Pinch.* I charge thee, Satan, housed within this man,
To yield possession to my holy prayers,
And to thy state of darkness hie thee straight;
I conjure thee by all the saints in heaven.

E. Antipholus. Peace, doting wizard, peace; I am not
mad.

60 *Adriana.* O, that thou wert not, poor distressèd soul!

E. Antipholus. You minion,° you, are these your cus-
tomers?
Did this companion° with the saffron° face
Revel and feast it at my house today,

42 **respice finem** (this proverbial phrase, which Dromio translates,
was sometimes punningly altered to *"respice funem,"* remember the
rope)   43 **parrot** (parrots were taught to cry "rope")   48 **conjurer**
(who can exorcise evil spirits, also called "Doctor" because of his
learning)   50 **please** satisfy   52 **ecstasy** frenzy   61 **minion** harlot
62 **companion** low fellow   62 **saffron** yellow

Whilst upon me the guilty doors were shut,
And I denied° to enter in my house?   65

Adriana. O, husband, God doth know you dined at
home,
Where would you had remained until this time,
Free from these slanders and this open shame!

E. Antipholus. Dined at home! Thou villain, what
sayest thou?

E. Dromio. Sir, sooth to say, you did not dine at
home.   70

E. Antipholus. Were not my doors locked up, and I
shut out?

E. Dromio. Perdie,° your doors were locked, and you
shut out.

E. Antipholus. And did not she herself revile me
there?

E. Dromio. Sans fable,° she herself reviled you there.

E. Antipholus. Did not her kitchen maid rail, taunt,
and scorn me?   75

E. Dromio. Certes,° she did; the kitchen vestal°
scorned you.

E. Antipholus. And did not I in rage depart from
thence?

E. Dromio. In verity, you did; my bones bears witness,
That since have felt the vigor of his rage.

Adriana. Is't good to soothe° him in these contraries?   80

Pinch. It is no shame; the fellow finds his vein,
And yielding to him humors well his frenzy.

---

65 **denied** not allowed   72 **Perdie** by God *("par Dieu")*   74 **Sans
able** without lying (French)   76 **Certes** certainly   76 **kitchen vestal**
so called, as Dr. Johnson pointed out, because she kept the fire
burning, like the vestal virgins of Rome)   80 **soothe** humor

E. Antipholus. Thou hast suborned° the goldsmith to
   arrest me.

Adriana. Alas, I sent you money to redeem you,
85   By Dromio here, who came in haste for it.

E. Dromio. Money by me? Heart and goodwill you
   might,
   But, surely, master, not a rag° of money.

E. Antipholus. Went'st not thou to her for a purse
   of ducats?

Adriana. He came to me, and I delivered it.

90 *Luciana.* And I am witness with her that she did.

E. Dromio. God and the rope-maker bear me witness
   That I was sent for nothing but a rope.

Pinch. Mistress, both man and master is possessed;
   I know it by their pale and deadly looks.
95   They must be bound, and laid in some dark room.

E. Antipholus. Say, wherefore didst thou lock me
   forth° today,
   And why dost thou deny the bag of gold?

Adriana. I did not, gentle husband, lock thee forth.

E. Dromio. And, gentle master, I received no gold;
100   But I confess, sir, that we were locked out.

Adriana. Dissembling villain, thou speak'st false in
   both.

E. Antipholus. Dissembling harlot, thou art false in
   all,
   And art confederate° with a damnèd pack°
   To make a loathsome abject scorn of me;
105   But with these nails I'll pluck out these false eyes
   That would behold in me this shameful sport.

      Enter three or four, and offer to bind him.
             He strives.

83 **suborned** colluded with   87 **rag** (slang for farthing) **96 forth**
out   103 **confederate** in conspiracy   103 **pack** gang of rogues

Adriana. O, bind him, bind him, let him not come
　near me!

Pinch. More company! The fiend is strong within him.

Luciana. Ay me,° poor man, how pale and wan he
　looks.

E. Antipholus. What, will you murder me? Thou
　jailer, thou,　　　　　　　　　　　　　　　　　　*110*
　I am thy prisoner; wilt thou suffer them
　To make a rescue?°

Officer.　　　　　　　　Masters, let him go.
　He is my prisoner, and you shall not have him.

Pinch. Go, bind this man, for he is frantic too.

Adriana. What wilt thou do, thou peevish° officer?　*115*
　Hast thou delight to see a wretched man
　Do outrage and displeasure° to himself?

Officer. He is my prisoner; if I let him go,
　The debt he owes will be required of me.

Adriana. I will discharge° thee ere I go from thee.　*120*
　Bear me forthwith unto his creditor,
　And, knowing how the debt grows, I will pay it.
　Good master doctor, see him safe conveyed
　Home to my house. O most unhappy° day!

E. Antipholus. O most unhappy strumpet!　　　　　*125*

E. Dromio. Master, I am here ent'red in bond for you.

E. Antipholus. Out on thee, villain! Wherefore dost
　thou mad° me?

E. Dromio. Will you be bound for nothing? Be mad,
　good master;
　Cry, "The devil!"

Luciana. God help, poor souls, how idly° do they
　talk!
　　　　　　　　　　　　　　　　　　　　　　　130

109 Ay me (expression of sympathy)　112 rescue deliverance by force
115 peevish stupid　117 displeasure offense　120 discharge pay
124 unhappy unfortunate　127 mad madden　130 idly foolishly

Adriana. Go bear him hence. Sister, go you with me.

*Exeunt [Pinch and others with Antipholus of
Ephesus and Dromio of Ephesus]. Manet° Officer,
Adriana, Luciana, Courtesan.*

Say now, whose suit is he arrested at?

Officer. One Angelo, a goldsmith, do you know him?

Adriana. I know the man. What is the sum he owes?

Officer. Two hundred ducats.

135 *Adriana.*   Say, how grows° it due?

Officer. Due for a chain your husband had of him.

Adriana. He did bespeak a chain for me, but had it
    not.

Courtesan. Whenas your husband, all in rage, today
    Came to my house, and took away my ring—
140 The ring I saw upon his finger now—
    Straight after did I meet him with a chain.

Adriana. It may be so, but I did never see it.
    Come, jailer, bring me where the goldsmith is;
    I long to know the truth hereof at large.

*Enter Antipholus of Syracuse, with his rapier
    drawn, and Dromio of Syracuse.*

145 *Luciana.* God for thy mercy, they are loose again.

Adriana. And come with naked° swords. Let's call
    more help
    To have them bound again.

Officer.   Away, they'll kill us!

*Run all out. Exeunt omnes as fast as may be,
    frighted.*

S. Antipholus. I see these witches are afraid of swords.

131s.d. **Manet** remains (Latin; third person singular, but common
with a plural subject) 135 **grows** comes 146 **naked** drawn

S. Dromio. She that would be your wife now ran from
   you.

S. Antipholus. Come to the Centaur; fetch our stuff°
   from thence.   150
   I long that we were safe and sound aboard.

S. Dromio. Faith, stay here this night; they will surely
   do us no harm. You saw they speak us fair, give
   us gold. Methinks they are such a gentle nation
   that, but for the mountain of mad flesh that claims 155
   marriage of me, I could find in my heart to stay here
   still,° and turn witch.

S. Antipholus. I will not stay tonight for all the town;
   Therefore away, to get our stuff aboard.   *Exeunt.*

150 **stuff** baggage   157 **still** always

ACT V

Scene I. [*Before the Phoenix.*]

Enter [Another] Merchant and [Angelo] the
Goldsmith.

Angelo. I am sorry, sir, that I have hind'red you;
But I protest he had the chain of me.
Though most dishonestly he doth deny it.

Merchant. How is the man esteemed here in the city?

5 *Angelo.* Of very reverend reputation, sir,
Of credit infinite, highly beloved,
Second to none that lives here in the city.
His word might bear° my wealth at any time.

Merchant. Speak softly; yonder, as I think, he walks.

Enter Antipholus and Dromio of Syracuse again.

10 *Angelo.* 'Tis so; and that self° chain about his neck,
Which he forswore° most monstrously to have.
Good sir, draw near to me; I'll speak to him.
Signor Antipholus, I wonder much
That you would put me to this shame and trouble,
15 And not without some scandal to yourself,
With circumstance° and oaths so to deny
This chain which now you wear so openly.

V.i.8 **bear** command the support of   10 **self** same   11 **forswore** denied on oath   16 **circumstance** detailed argument

Beside the charge,° the shame, imprisonment,
You have done wrong to this my honest friend,
Who, but for staying on our controversy,   20
Had hoisted sail and put to sea today.
This chain you had of me, can you deny it?

S. Antipholus. I think I had; I never did deny it.

Merchant. Yes, that you did, sir, and forswore it too.

S. Antipholus. Who heard me to deny it or forswear
it?   25

Merchant. These ears of mine, thou know'st, did hear
thee.
Fie on thee, wretch! 'Tis pity that thou liv'st
To walk where any honest men resort.

S. Antipholus. Thou art a villain to impeach° me thus.
I'll prove mine honor and mine honesty   30
Against thee presently,° if thou dar'st stand.°

Merchant. I dare, and do defy thee for a villain!

They draw. Enter Adriana, Luciana, Courtesan,
and others.

Adriana. Hold, hurt him not, for God's sake! He is
mad.
Some get within him,° take his sword away.
Bind Dromio too, and bear them to my house.   35

S. Dromio. Run, master, run; for God's sake, take a
house!°
This is some priory. In, or we are spoiled.
                              Exeunt to the Priory.

          Enter Lady Abbess.

Abbess. Be quiet, people. Wherefore throng you
hither?

Adriana. To fetch my poor distracted husband hence.

---

18 **charge** expense   29 **impeach** accuse   31 **presently** at once   31
stand prepare to fight   34 **within him** inside his guard   36 **take a**
house get inside

40   Let us come in, that we may bind him fast,
    And bear him home for his recovery.

Angelo. I knew he was not in his perfect wits.

Merchant. I am sorry now that I did draw on him.

Abbess. How long hath this possession° held the man?

45 *Adriana.* This week he hath been heavy, sour, sad,
    And much different from the man he was;
    But till this afternoon his passion
    Ne'er brake into extremity of rage.

Abbess. Hath he not lost much wealth by wrack of
    sea?°
50 Buried some dear friend? Hath not else his eye
    Strayed° his affection in unlawful love—
    A sin prevailing much in youthful men,
    Who give their eyes the liberty of gazing?
    Which of these sorrows is he subject to?

55 *Adriana.* To none of these, except it be the last,
    Namely, some love that drew him oft from home.

Abbess. You should for that have reprehended him.

Adriana. Why, so I did.

Abbess.   Ay, but not rough enough.

Adriana. As roughly as my modesty would let me.

Abbess. Haply, in private.

60 *Adriana.*   And in assemblies too.

Abbess. Ay, but not enough.

Adriana. It was the copy° of our conference.
    In bed he slept not for° my urging it;
    At board he fed not for my urging it;
65 Alone, it was the subject of my theme:
    In company I often glancèd° it;
    Still° did I tell him it was vile and bad.

---

44 **possession** (by evil spirits)   49 **wrack of sea** shipwreck   51 **Strayed** led astray   62 **copy** topic   63 **for** because of   66 **glancèd** touched on   67 **Still** continually

Abbess. And thereof came it that the man was mad.
  The venom° clamors of a jealous woman
  Poisons more deadly than a mad dog's tooth.   *70*
  It seems his sleeps were hind'red by thy railing,
  And thereof comes it that his head is light.
  Thou say'st his meat was sauced with thy upbraid-
    ings;
  Unquiet meals make ill digestions;
  Thereof the raging fire of fever bred—   *75*
  And what's a fever but a fit of madness?
  Thou sayest his sports were hind'red by thy brawls;
  Sweet recreation barred, what doth ensue
  But moody and dull melancholy,
  Kinsman to grim and comfortless despair,   *80*
  And at her heels a huge infectious troop
  Of pale distemperatures° and foes to life?
  In food, in sport, and life-preserving rest
  To be disturbed, would mad° or man or beast.
  The consequence is, then, thy jealous fits   *85*
  Hath scared thy husband from the use of wits.

Luciana. She never reprehended him but mildly,
  When he demeaned° himself rough, rude, and
    wildly.
  Why bear you these rebukes and answer not?

Adriana. She did betray me to my own reproof.°   *90*
  Good people, enter and lay hold on him.

Abbess. No, not a creature enters in my house.

Adriana. Then, let your servants bring my husband
  forth.

Abbess. Neither. He took this place for sanctuary,°
  And it shall privilege him° from your hands   *95*
  Till I have brought him to his wits again,
  Or lose my labor in assaying° it.

69 **venom** venomous   82 **distemperatures** disorders   84 **mad** madden   88 **demeaned** conducted   90 **my own reproof** self-accusation
94 **sanctuary** right of asylum   95 **privilege him** grant him immunity
97 **assaying** attempting

Adriana. I will attend my husband, be his nurse,
    Diet his sickness, for it is my office,
100   And will have no attorney° but myself;
    And therefore let me have him home with me.

Abbess. Be patient, for I will not let him stir
    Till I have used the approvèd° means I have,
    With wholesome syrups, drugs, and holy prayers,
105   To make of him a formal° man again.
    It is a branch and parcel° of mine oath,
    A charitable duty of my order;
    Therefore depart, and leave him here with me.

Adriana. I will not hence, and leave my husband here;
110   And ill it doth beseem your holiness
    To separate the husband and the wife.

Abbess. Be quiet and depart, thou shalt not have him.
                              [Exit.]

Luciana. Complain unto the Duke of this indignity.

Adriana. Come, go. I will fall prostrate at his feet,
115   And never rise until my tears and prayers
    Have won his Grace to come in person hither,
    And take perforce my husband from the Abbess.

Merchant. By this, I think, the dial points at five:
    Anon, I'm sure, the Duke himself in person
120   Comes this way to the melancholy vale,
    The place of death and sorry° execution,
    Behind the ditches of the abbey here.

Angelo. Upon what cause?

Merchant. To see a reverend Syracusian merchant,
125   Who put unluckily into this bay
    Against the laws and statutes of this town,
    Beheaded publicly for his offense.

Angelo. See, where they come. We will behold his
    death.

100 **attorney** agent   103 **approvèd** tested   105 **formal** normal   106
branch and parcel part and parcel   121 **sorry** sorrowful

uciana. Kneel to the Duke before he pass the abbey.

*Enter the Duke of Ephesus and [Egeon] the
Merchant of Syracuse, barehead, with the Heads-
man and other Officers.*

Duke. Yet once again proclaim it publicly,   130
  If any friend will pay the sum for him,
  He shall not die; so much we tender° him.

Adriana. Justice, most sacred Duke, against the
    Abbess!

Duke. She is a virtuous and a reverend lady.
  It cannot be that she hath done thee wrong.   135

Adriana. May it please your Grace, Antipholus, my
    husband,
  Who I made lord of me and all I had
  At your important° letters, this ill day
  A most outrageous fit of madness took him:
  That° desp'rately he hurried through the street,   140
  With him his bondman° all as mad as he,
  Doing displeasure° to the citizens
  By rushing in their houses, bearing thence
  Rings, jewels, anything his rage did like.
  Once did I get him bound, and sent him home,   145
  Whilst to take order° for the wrongs I went,
  That here and there his fury had committed.
  Anon, I wot° not by what strong° escape,
  He broke from those that had the guard of him,
  And with his mad attendant and himself,   150
  Each one with ireful passion, with drawn swords,
  Met us again and, madly bent on us,
  Chased us away, till, raising of more aid,
  We came again to bind them. Then they fled
  Into this abbey, whither we pursued them;   155
  And here the Abbess shuts the gates on us,
  And will not suffer us to fetch him out,
  Nor send him forth that we may bear him hence.

32 tender regard   138 important pressing   140 That so that   141
ondman slave   142 displeasure harm   146 take order settle
48 wot know   148 strong violent

Therefore, most gracious Duke, with thy command
160 Let him be brought forth and borne hence for help.

Duke. Long since thy husband served me in my wars,
And I to thee engaged a prince's word,
When thou didst make him master of thy bed,
To do him all the grace and good I could.
165 Go, some of you, knock at the abbey gate,
And bid the Lady Abbess come to me.
I will determine this before I stir.

Enter a Messenger.

Messenger. O mistress, mistress, shift and save your-
self.
My master and his man are both broke loose,
170 Beaten the maids a-row,° and bound the doctor,
Whose beard they have singed off with brands of
fire,
And ever as it blazed, they threw on him
Great pails of puddled° mire to quench the hair.
My master preaches patience to him, and the while
175 His man with scissors nicks him like a fool;°
And, sure, unless you send some present help,
Between them they will kill the conjurer.

Adriana. Peace, fool, thy master and his man are here,
And that is false thou dost report to us.

180 *Messenger.* Mistress, upon my life, I tell you true;
I have not breathed almost° since I did see it.
He cries for you and vows, if he can take you,
To scorch your face and to disfigure you.

Cry within.

Hark, hark! I hear him, mistress. Fly, begone.

Duke. Come, stand by me; fear nothing. Guard with
185 halberds!°

170 **a-row** one after another 173 **puddled** muddied 175 **fool** (Elizabethan fools had their hair cut off) 181 **not breathed almost** hardly
breathed 185 **halberds** (poles with heads like battle-axes)

Adriana. Ay me, it is my husband! Witness you,
  That he is borne about invisible.
  Even now we housed him° in the abbey here,
  And now he's there, past thought of human rea-
    son.

Enter Antipholus and Dromio of Ephesus.

E. Antipholus. Justice, most gracious Duke! O, grant
  me justice,   190
  Even for the service that long since I did thee,
  When I bestrid° thee in the wars, and took
  Deep scars to save thy life; even for the blood
  That then I lost for thee, now grant me justice.

Egeon. Unless the fear of death doth make me dote, 195
  I see my son Antipholus and Dromio.

E. Antipholus. Justice, sweet Prince, against that
  woman there!
  She whom thou gav'st to me to be my wife;
  That hath abusèd and dishonored me,
  Even in the strength and height° of injury: 200
  Beyond imagination is the wrong
  That she this day hath shameless thrown on me.

Duke. Discover° how, and thou shalt find me just.

E. Antipholus. This day, great Duke, she shut the
  doors upon me,
  While she with harlots° feasted in my house.   205

Duke. A grievous fault. Say, woman, didst thou so?

Adriana. No, my good lord. Myself, he, and my sister
  Today did dine together; so befall my soul
  As this is false he burdens me withal.°

Luciana. Ne'er may I look on day, nor sleep on night,° 210
  But she tells to your Highness simple truth.

---

188 **housed him** pursued him to shelter   192 **bestrid** defended by
standing over   200 **in the strength and height** to the strongest degree   203 **Discover** reveal   205 **harlots** rascals   208–09 **so befall
. . . me withal** i.e., I stake my soul that what he charges me with is
false   210 **on night** at night

Angelo. O perjured woman! They are both forsworn.
    In this the madman justly chargeth them.

E. Antipholus. My liege, I am advisèd° what I say,
215 Neither disturbed with the effect of wine,
    Nor heady-rash, provoked with raging ire,
    Albeit my wrongs might make one wiser mad.
    This woman locked me out this day from dinner.
    That goldsmith there, were he not packed° with
        her,
220 Could witness it; for he was with me then,
    Who parted with me to go fetch a chain,
    Promising to bring it to the Porpentine,
    Where Balthasar and I did dine together.
    Our dinner done, and he not coming thither,
225 I went to seek him. In the street I met him,
    And in his company that gentleman.
    There did this perjured goldsmith swear me down
    That I this day of him received the chain,
    Which, God he knows, I saw not; for the which,
230 He did arrest me with an officer.
    I did obey, and sent my peasant° home
    For certain ducats; he with none returned.
    Then fairly I bespoke° the officer
    To go in person with me to my house.
235 By th' way we met
    My wife, her sister, and a rabble more
    Of vile confederates. Along with them
    They brought one Pinch, a hungry lean-faced vil-
        lain;
    A mere anatomy,° a mountebank,
240 A threadbare juggler° and a fortune-teller,
    A needy-hollow-eyed-sharp-looking wretch;
    A living dead man. This pernicious slave,
    Forsooth, took on him as° a conjurer;
    And, gazing in mine eyes, feeling my pulse,

---

214 **advisèd** well aware of   219 **packed** conspiring   231 **peasant**
bondman   233 **fairly I bespoke** politely I addressed   239 **mere
anatomy** sheer skeleton   240 **juggler** sorcerer   243 **took on him as**
assumed the part of

And with no face, as 'twere, out-facing me,   245
Cries out, I was possessed. Then all together
They fell upon me, bound me, bore me thence,
And in a dark and dankish vault at home
There left me and my man, both bound together,
Till gnawing with my teeth my bonds in sunder,°   250
I gained my freedom; and immediately
Ran hither to your Grace, whom I beseech
To give me ample satisfaction
For these deep shames and great indignities.

Angelo. My lord, in truth, thus far I witness with him: 255
That he dined not at home, but was locked out.

Duke. But had he such a chain of thee, or no?

Angelo. He had, my lord, and when he ran in here
These people saw the chain about his neck.

Merchant. Besides, I will be sworn these ears of mine   260
Heard you confess you had the chain of him,
After you first forswore it on the Mart;
And, thereupon, I drew my sword on you;
And then you fled into this abbey here,
From whence, I think, you are come by miracle.   265

E. Antipholus. I never came within these abbey walls,
Nor ever didst thou draw thy sword on me.
I never saw the chain, so help me Heaven!
And this is false you burden me withal.

Duke. Why, what an intricate impeach° is this!   270
I think you all have drunk of Circe's cup.°
If here you housed him, here he would have been;
If he were mad, he would not plead so coldly.°
You say he dined at home, the goldsmith here
Denies that saying. Sirrah, what say you?   275

E. Dromio. Sir, he dined with her there at the Porpentine.

---

250 **in sunder** asunder   270 **impeach** accusation   271 **Circe's cup**
(potion which, in Greek mythology, turns men into beasts)   273
coldly rationally

Courtesan. He did, and from my finger snatched that
    ring.

E. Antipholus. 'Tis true, my liege, this ring I had of
    her.

Duke. Saw'st thou him enter at the abbey here?

280 *Courtesan.* As sure, my liege, as I do see your Grace.

Duke. Why, this is strange. Go call the Abbess hither.
    I think you are all mated,° or stark mad.
                        Exit One to the Abbey.

Egeon. Most mighty Duke, vouchsafe me° speak a
    word.
    Haply° I see a friend will save my life,
285   And pay the sum that may deliver me.

Duke. Speak freely, Syracusian, what thou wilt.

Egeon. Is not your name, sir, called Antipholus?
    And is not that your bondman Dromio?

E. Dromio. Within this hour I was his bondman, sir,
290   But he, I thank him, gnawed in two my cords.
    Now am I Dromio, and his man, unbound.

Egeon. I am sure you both of you remember me.

E. Dromio. Ourselves we do remember, sir, by you;
    For lately we were bound,° as you are now.
295   You are not Pinch's patient, are you, sir?

Egeon. Why look you strange on me? You know me
    well.

E. Antipholus. I never saw you in my life till now.

Egeon. O, grief hath changed me since you saw me
    last,
    And careful° hours with time's deformèd hand
300   Have written strange defeatures° in my face.

---

282 **mated** confounded   283 **vouchsafe me** allow me to   284 **Haply**
perchance   294 **bound** (pun on being a bondservant and being
literally bound as a madman)   299 **careful** full of care   300 **defeatures** disfigurements

But tell me yet, dost thou not know my voice?

E. Antipholus. Neither.

Egeon. Dromio, nor thou?

E. Dromio.   No, trust me, sir, nor I.

Egeon. I am sure thou dost!

E. Dromio. Ay, sir, but I am sure I do not; and what-   305
    soever a man denies, you are now bound° to believe
    him.

Egeon. Not know my voice! O, time's extremity,
    Hast thou so cracked and splitted my poor tongue
    In seven short years, that here my only son   310
    Knows not my feeble key of untuned cares?°
    Though now this grainèd° face of mine be hid
    In sap-consuming winter's drizzled snow,
    And all the conduits of my blood froze up,
    Yet hath my night of life some memory;   315
    My wasting lamps° some fading glimmer left;
    My dull deaf ears a little use to hear.
    All these old witnesses—I cannot err—
    Tell me thou art my son Antipholus.

E. Antipholus. I never saw my father in my life.   320

Egeon. But seven years since, in Syracusa, boy,
    Thou know'st we parted; but perhaps, my son,
    Thou sham'st to acknowledge me in misery.

E. Antipholus. The Duke and all that know me in the
    city
    Can witness with me that it is not so.   325
    I ne'er saw Syracusa in my life.

Duke. I tell thee, Syracusian, twenty years
    Have I been patron to Antipholus,
    During which time he ne'er saw Syracusa.   330
    I see thy age and dangers make thee dote.

---

306 **bound** (a further quibble)   311 **feeble key of untuned cares**
voice enfeebled by discordant cares   312 **grainèd** furrowed   316
wasting lamps dimming eyes

*Enter the Abbess with Antipholus of Syracuse
and Dromio of Syracuse.*

Abbess. Most mighty Duke, behold a man much
    wronged.   *All gather to see them.*

Adriana. I see two husbands, or mine eyes deceive me.

Duke. One of these men is genius° to the other;
    And so of these, which is the natural man,
335   And which the spirit? Who deciphers them?

S. Dromio. I, sir, am Dromio; command him away.

E. Dromio. I, sir, am Dromio; pray let me stay.

S. Antipholus. Egeon art thou not, or else his ghost?

S. Dromio. O, my old master! Who hath bound him
    here?

340 *Abbess.* Whoever bound him, I will loose his bonds,
    And gain a husband by his liberty.
    Speak, old Egeon, if thou beest the man
    That hadst a wife once called Emilia,
    That bore thee at a burden° two fair sons!
345   O, if thou beest the same Egeon, speak;
    And speak unto the same Emilia.

Duke. [*Aside*] Why, here begins his morning story
    right:
    These two Antipholus', these two so like,
    And these two Dromios, one in semblance,°
350   Besides her urging° of her wrack at sea;
    These are the parents to these children,
    Which accidentally are met together.

Egeon. If I dream not, thou art Emilia.
    If thou art she, tell me where is that son
355   That floated with thee on the fatal raft?

Abbess. By men of Epidamnum, he and I
    And the twin Dromio, all were taken up;

333 **genius** attendant spirit   344 **burden** birth   349 **semblance** appearance   350 **urging** account

But by and by rude fishermen of Corinth
By force took Dromio and my son from them,
And me they left with those of Epidamnum.   *360*
What then became of them, I cannot tell;
I to° this fortune that you see me in.

Duke. Antipholus, thou cam'st from Corinth first.

S. Antipholus. No, sir, not I; I came from Syracuse.

Duke. Stay, stand apart; I know not which is which.   *365*

E. Antipholus. I came from Corinth, my most gracious lord.

E. Dromio. And I with him.

E. Antipholus. Brought to this town by that most
famous warrior,
Duke Menaphon, your most renownèd uncle.

Adriana. Which of you two did dine with me today?   *370*

S. Antipholus. I, gentle mistress.

Adriana.   And are not you my husband?

E. Antipholus. No, I say nay to that.

S. Antipholus. And so do I, yet did she call me so;
And this fair gentlewoman, her sister here,
Did call me brother. What I told you then   *375*
I hope I shall have leisure to make good,
If this be not a dream I see and hear.

Angelo. That is the chain, sir, which you had of me.

S. Antipholus. I think it be, sir; I deny it not.

E. Antipholus. And you, sir, for this chain arrested
me.   *380*

Angelo. I think I did, sir. I deny it not.

Adriana. I sent you money, sir, to be your bail,
By Dromio; but I think he brought it not.

E. Dromio. No, none by me.

362 **I to** I came to

S. Antipholus. This purse of ducats I received from
385   you,
And Dromio, my man, did bring them me.
I see we still° did meet each other's man,
And I was ta'en for him, and he for me,
And thereupon these errors are arose.

E. Antipholus. These ducats pawn I for my father
390   here.

Duke. It shall not need; thy father hath his life.

Courtesan. Sir, I must have that diamond from you.

E. Antipholus. There, take it, and much thanks for
      my good cheer.

Abbess. Renownèd Duke, vouchsafe to take the pains
395   To go with us into the abbey here,
And hear at large discoursèd all our fortunes;
And all that are assembled in this place,
That by this sympathizèd° one day's error
Have suffered wrong, go, keep us company,
400   And we shall make full satisfaction.
Thirty-three years have I but gone in travail°
Of you, my sons, and till this present hour
My heavy burden ne'er delivered.
The Duke, my husband, and my children both,
405   And you the calendars° of their nativity,
Go to a gossips'° feast, and joy with me
After so long grief such nativity.°

Duke. With all my heart I'll gossip° at this feast.
              Exeunt [all except] the two Dromios
              and two Brothers.

S. Dromio. Master, shall I fetch your stuff from ship-
      board?

---

387 **still** repeatedly   398 **sympathizèd** shared   401 **travail** child-
birth (with a pun on "travel")   405 **calendars** (the Dromios mark
the age of the Antipholuses)   406 **gossips** godparents   407 **nativity**
a christening party (suggested emendations are "festivity" and
"felicity")   408 **gossip** make merry

E. *Antipholus*. Dromio, what stuff of mine hast thou
embarked?   *410*

S. *Dromio*. Your goods that lay at host,° sir, in the
Centaur.

S. *Antipholus*. He speaks to me. I am your master,
Dromio.
Come, go with us; we'll look to that anon.
Embrace thy brother there; rejoice with him.
                    Exit [with Antipholus of Ephesus].

S. *Dromio*. There is a fat friend at your master's
house,   *415*
That kitchened° me for you today at dinner;
She now shall be my sister, not my wife.

E. *Dromio*. Methinks you are my glass, and not my
brother;
I see by you I am a sweet-faced° youth.
Will you walk in to see their gossiping?   *420*

S. *Dromio*. Not I, sir, you are my elder.

E. *Dromio*. That's a question; how shall we try it?

S. *Dromio*. We'll draw cuts for the senior; till then,
lead thou first.

E. *Dromio*. Nay, then, thus: *425*
We came into the world like brother and brother:
And now let's go hand in hand, not one before
another.   *Exeunt.*

                        FINIS

411 at host in the care of the host   416 kitchened entertained in the
kitchen   419 sweet-faced good-looking

Textual Note

The Comedy of Errors was first published in the Folio of 1623, which provides the only authoritative text. It is possible that the copy for the Folio was Shakespeare's manuscript; the ambiguity of some names in stage directions and in speech prefixes would have been confusing in a promptbook. For example, Egeon is *Mer(chant)* in I.i., but other merchants appear in other scenes without distinctive titles. More important, *E. Dro(mio)* is, as might be expected, *Dromio of Ephesus;* but *E. Ant.* is Antipholus of Syracuse, an abbreviation of his earlier designation, *Ant. Errotis*—which is perhaps an approximation of *erraticus,* wandering. A promptbook doubtless would have clarified the nomenclature.

The Folio's text is a good one, presenting the editor with relatively few problems. In the present edition the speech prefixes and names in stage directions have been regularized, spelling and punctuation have been modernized, and obvious typographical errors have been corrected. A few passages that the Folio prints as prose are given in verse, and the positions of a few stage directions have been slightly altered. Act division (translated from the Latin) is that of the Folio; scene division is that of the Globe text. Other departures from the Folio are listed below, with the adopted reading first, in italics, and the original reading next, in roman.

I.i.17 *at* at any   42 *the* he   102 *upon* vp   116 *bark* backe   123 *thee* they   151 *health* helpe

I.ii.s.d. *Antipholus of Syracuse* Antipholis Erotes   4 *arrival* a riuall
80 *lose* loose   32s.d. *Exit* Exeunt   40 *unhappy* vnhappie a   65 *score*
scoure   66 *clock* cooke   93 *God's* God   94s.d. *Exit* Exeunt

II.i.s.d. *Antipholus of Ephesus* Antipholis Sereptus   11 *o' door* adore
42 *ill* thus   45 *two* too   61 *thousand* hundred   72 *errand* arrant
107 *alone, alone* alone, a loue   112 *Wear* Where   113 *But* By

II.ii.s.d. *Antipholus of Syracuse* Antipholis Errotis   12 *didst* did
didst   80 *men* them   98 *tiring* trying   102 *e'en* in   176 *stronger*
stranger   187 *offered* free'd   195 *drone* Dromio   196 *am not I*
am I not

III.i.54 *trow* hope   75 *you* your   89 *her* your   91 *her* your

III.ii.s.d. *Luciana* Iuliana   1 *Luciana* Iulia   2 *Antipholus, hate* An-
ipholus   4 *building* buildings   16 *attaint* attaine   21 *but* not   26 *wife*
wise   46 *sister's* sister   49 *bed* bud   49 *them* thee   57 *where* when
111 *and* is   129 *chalky* chalkle   171 *here is* here's

IV.i.17 *her* their   28 *carat* charect   47 *to blame* too blame   88 *then
she* then sir she

IV.ii.6 *Of* Oh   60 *'a* I

IV.iii.1 *S. Antipholus* [F omits]   62 *if you do* if do

V.i.s.d. *Another Merchant* the Merchant   33 *God's* God   121 *death*
depth   168 *Messenger* [F omits]   246 *all together* altogether
282s.d. *Abbey* Abbesse   403 *ne'er* are   406 *joy with* go with
408s.d. *Exeunt* Exeunt omnes. Manet   423 *senior* Signior

The Source of
The Comedy of Errors

Titus Maccius Plautus, who was born during the third century B.C. and died during the second, was the most popular of the Roman playwrights. Freely adapted into the Latin vernacular from the New Comedy of the Greeks, his plays were distinguished by their broad humor, fast movement, vivid language, and nimble versification. Among the twenty-one Plautine comedies that have come down to us, the *Menaechmi* is one of the best known and the most influential, doubtless because it reduces the dilemmas of mistaken identity to an archetypal pattern. The Elizabethan translation, which Shakespeare may or may not have known in some form, was published in 1595, presumably a few years after the first production of *The Comedy of Errors*. The initials of the translator, W.W., are generally thought to stand for William Warner, a man of letters who is sometimes remembered for his historical poem, *Albion's England*. His prose version of Plautus' comedy is rough, lively, and actable. Occasionally it substitutes a colloquial turn of phrase for a literal expression that would sound pedantic. Though it does not translate the prologue, which sets the scene and recapitulates the plot, it does begin with the synopsis in verse (added to Plautus by a later hand), which originally took the form of an acrostic spelling the title of the play. For the underplot of the twin servants, Shakespeare is indebted to the *Amphitruo* of Plautus, particularly the opening scene and the fourth act.

A Pleasant and Fine Conceited Comedy
Called *Menaechmus,*
Taken Out of the Most Excellent Poet
Plautus.

THE ARGUMENT

Two twin-born sons a Sicil merchant had:
Menaechmus one, and Sosicles the other.
The first his father lost, a little lad;
The grandsire named the latter like his brother.
This, grown a man, long travel took to seek
His brother, and to Epidamnum came,
Where th'other dwelt enriched, and him so like
That citizens there take him for the same.
Father, wife, neighbors, each mistaking either,
Much pleasant error, ere they meet together.

Act I. Scene I.

Enter Peniculus, a Parasite.

[*Peniculus.*] Peniculus was given me for my name
when I was young, because like a broom I swept
all clean away, wheresoe'er I be come: namely all
the victuals which are set before me. Now, in my
judgment, men that clap iron bolts on such cap-
tives as they would keep safe, and tie those servants
in chains who they think will run away, they com-

mit an exceeding great folly. My reason is: these
poor wretches, enduring one misery upon another,
never cease devising how, by wrenching asunder
their gyves or by some subtlety or other, they may
escape such cursed bonds. If, then, ye would keep
a man without all suspicion of running away from
ye, the surest way is to tie him with meat, drink,
and ease. Let him ever be idle, eat his bellyful, and
carouse while his skin will hold, and he shall never,
I warrant ye, stir a foot. These strings to tie one by
the teeth pass all the bands of iron, steel, or what
metal soever; for, the more slack and easy ye make
them, the faster shall they tie the party which is in
them. I speak this upon experience of myself, who
am now going for Menaechmus, there willingly to
be tied to his good cheer. He is commonly so exceeding bountiful and liberal in his fare, as no marvel though such guests as myself be drawn to his
table and tied there in his dishes. Now because I
have lately been a stranger there, I mean to visit
him at dinner; for my stomach, methinks, even
thrusts me into the fetters of his dainty fare. But
yonder I [see] his door open, and himself ready to
come forth.

Scene II.

*Enter Menaechmus, talking back to his Wife
within.*

[*Menaechmus.*] If ye were not such a brabbling fool
and mad-brain scold as ye are, ye would never thus
cross your husband in all actions. 'Tis no matter;
let her serve me thus once more, I'll send her home
to her dad with a vengeance. I can never go forth
a-doors but she asketh me whither I go, what I do,
what business, what I fetch, what I carry, as though
she were a constable or a toll-gatherer. I have pam-

pered her too much; she hath servants about her,
wool, flax, and all things necessary to busy her
withal; yet she watcheth and wondreth whither I
go. Well, sith it is so, she shall now have some
cause; I mean to dine this day abroad with a sweet
friend of mine.

Peniculus. Yea, marry, now comes he to the point
that pricks me: this last speech galls me as much
as it would do his wife. If he dine not at home, I
am dressed.

Menaechmus. We that have loves abroad and wives
at home are miserably hampered; yet would every
man could tame his shrew as well as I do mine!
I have now filched away a fine riding cloak of my
wife's, which I mean to bestow upon one that I
love better. Nay, if she be so wary and watchful
over me, I count it an alms-deed to deceive her.

Peniculus. Come, what share have I in that same?

Menaechmus. Out alas! I am taken.

Peniculus. True, but by your friend.

Menaechmus. What, mine own Peniculus?

Peniculus. Yours, i' faith, body and goods—if I had
any.

Menaechmus. Why, thou hast a body.

Peniculus. Yea, but neither goods nor good body.

Menaechmus. Thou couldst never come fitter in all
thy life.

Peniculus. Tush, I ever do so to my friends; I know
how to come always in the nick. Where dine ye
today?

Menaechmus. I'll tell thee of a notable prank.

Peniculus. What, did the cook mar your meat in the
dressing? Would I might see the reversion.

Menaechmus. Tell me didst thou see a picture how

Jupiter's eagle snatched away Ganymede, or how Venus stole away Adonis?

Peniculus. Often; but what care I for shadows? I want substance.

Menaechmus. Look thee here, look not I like such a picture?

Peniculus. O ho! What cloak have ye got here?

Menaechmus. Prithee say I am now a brave fellow.

Peniculus. But hark ye, where shall we dine?

Menaechmus. Tush, say as I bid thee, man.

Peniculus. Out of doubt, ye are a fine man.

Menaechmus. What, canst add nothing of thine own?

Peniculus. Ye are a most pleasant gentleman.

Menaechmus. On yet.

Peniculus. Nay, not a word more, unless ye tell me how you and your wife be fallen out.

Menaechmus. Nay I have a greater secret than that to impart to thee.

Peniculus. Say your mind.

Menaechmus. Come farther this way from my house.

Peniculus. So, let me hear.

Menaechmus. Nay, farther yet.

Peniculus. I warrant ye, man.

Menaechmus. Nay, yet farther.

Peniculus. 'Tis pity ye were not made a water-man to row in a wherry.

Menaechmus. Why?

Peniculus. Because ye go one way and look another still, lest your wife should follow ye. But what's the matter? Is't not almost dinnertime?

Menaechmus. Seest thou this cloak?

Peniculus. Not yet. Well, what of it?

Menaechmus. This same I mean to give to Erotium.

Peniculus. That's well, but what of all this?

Menaechmus. There I mean to have a delicious dinner prepared for her and me.

Peniculus. And me?

Menaechmus. And thee.

Peniculus. O sweet word! What, shall I knock presently at her door?

Menaechmus. Aye, knock. But stay too, Peniculus, let's not be too rash. Oh see, she is in good time coming forth.

Peniculus. Ah, he now looks against the sun; how her beams dazzle his eyes!

Enter Erotium.

Erotium. What, mine own Menaechmus! Welcome, sweetheart.

Peniculus. And what am I? Welcome too?

Erotium. You, sir? Ye are out of the number of my welcome guests.

Peniculus. I am like a voluntary soldier, out of pay.

Menaechmus. Erotium, I have determined that here shall be pitched a field this day; we mean to drink for the heavens; and which of us performs the bravest service at his weapon, the wine bowl, yourself as captain shall pay him his wages according to his deserts.

Erotium. Agreed.

Peniculus. I would we had the weapons, for my valor pricks me to the battle.

Menaechmus. Shall I tell thee, sweet mouse? I never

look upon thee, but I am quite out of love with my
wife.

Erotium. Yet ye cannot choose but ye must still wear
something of hers. What's this same?

Menaechmus. This? Such a spoil, sweetheart, as I took
from her to put on thee.

Erotium. Mine own Menaechmus, well worthy to be
my dear of all dearest!

Peniculus. Now she shows herself in her likeness;
when she finds him in the giving vein, she draws
close to him.

Menaechmus. I think Hercules got not the garter from
Hippolyta so hardly as I got this from my wife.
Take this, and with the same take my heart.

Peniculus. Thus they must do that are right lovers—
especially if they mean to [be] beggars with any
speed.

Menaechmus. I bought this same of late for my wife;
it stood me, I think, in some ten pound.

Peniculus. There's ten pound bestowed very thriftily.

Menaechmus. But know ye what I would have ye do?

Erotium. It shall be done: your dinner shall be ready.

Menaechmus. Let a good dinner be made for us three.
Hark ye, some oysters, a marrowbone pie or two,
some artichokes, and potato roots; let our other
dishes be as you please.

Erotium. You shall, sir.

Menaechmus. I have a little business in this city; by
that time dinner will be prepared. Farewell till then,
sweet Erotium. Come, Peniculus.

Peniculus. Nay, I mean to follow ye. I will sooner lose
my life than sight of you till this dinner be done.

                                              Exeunt.

Erotium. Who's there? Call me Cylindrus, the cook, hither.

Enter Cylindrus.

Cylindrus, take the handbasket; and here, there's ten shillings, is there not?

Cylindrus. 'Tis so, mistress.

Erotium. Buy me of all the daintiest meats ye can get, ye know what I mean, so as three may dine passing well, and yet no more than enough.

Cylindrus. What guests have ye today, mistress?

Erotium. Here will be Menaechmus and his parasite and myself.

Cylindrus. That's ten persons in all.

Erotium. How many?

Cylindrus. Ten; for I warrant you, that parasite may stand for eight at his victuals.

Erotium. Go, dispatch as I bid you, and look ye return with all speed.

Cylindrus. I will have all ready with a trice.

Exeunt.

Act II. Scene I.

Enter Menaechmus Sosicles [i.e., the Traveler], Messenio his servant, and some Sailors.

Menaechmus. Surely, Messenio, I think seafarers never take so comfortable a joy in anything as when they have been long tossed and turmoiled in the wide seas, they hap at last to ken land.

Messenio. I'll be sworn, I should not be gladder to see a whole country of mine own than I have been at such a sight. But, I pray, wherefore are we now

come to Epidamnum? Must we needs go to see
every town that we hear of?

Menaechmus. Till I find my brother, all towns are
alike to me. I must try in all places.

Messenio. Why, then, let's even as long as we live seek
your brother. Six years now have we roamed about
thus: Istria, Hispania, Massilia, Illyria, all the upper sea, all high Greece, all haven towns in Italy.
I think if we had sought a needle all this time, we
must needs have found it, had it been above
ground. It cannot be that he is alive; and to seek
a dead man thus among the living, what folly is it!

Menaechmus. Yea, could I but once find any man
that could certainly inform me of his death, I were
satisfied; otherwise I can never desist seeking. Little
knowest thou, Messenio, how near my heart it goes.

Messenio. This is washing of a blackamore. Faith,
let's go home, unless ye mean we should write a
story of our travel.

Menaechmus. Sirrah, no more of these saucy speeches!
I perceive I must teach ye how to serve me, not to
rule me.

Messenio. Aye so, now it appears what it is to be a
servant. Well, yet I must speak my conscience. Do
ye hear, sir? Faith, I must tell ye one thing: when
I look into the lean estate of your purse, and consider advisedly of your decaying stock, I hold it
very needful to be drawing homeward, lest in looking your brother, we quite lose ourselves. For this
assure yourself: this town, Epidamnum, is a place
of outrageous expenses, exceeding in all riot and
lasciviousness; and, I hear, as full of ribalds, parasites, drunkards, catchpoles, coney-catchers, and
sycophants as it can hold; then for courtesans, why
here's the currentest stamp of them in the world.
Ye must not think here to scape with as light cost
as in other places. The very name shows the nature:
no man comes hither *sine damno.*

Menaechmus. Ye say very well indeed. Give me my purse into mine own keeping, because I will so be the safer, *sine damno.*

Messenio. Why, sir?

Menaechmus. Because I fear you will be busy among the courtesans, and so be cozened of it. Then should I take great pains in belaboring your shoulders; so, to avoid both these harms, I'll keep it myself.

Messenio. I pray do so, sir; all the better.

Enter Cylindrus.

[*Cylindrus.*] I have tickling gear here, i' faith, for their dinners. It grieves me to the heart to think how that cormorant knave, Peniculus, must have his share in these dainty morsels. But what? Is Menaechmus come already, before I could come from the market? Menaechmus, how do ye, sir? How haps it ye come so soon?

Menaechmus. Godamercy, my good friend, dost thou know me?

Cylindrus. Know ye? No, not I. Where's Mouldy-chaps that must dine with ye? A murrain on his manners!

Menaechmus. Whom meanest thou, good fellow?

Cylindrus. Why, Peniculus, worship, that whoreson lick-trencher, your parasitical attendant.

Menaechmus. What Peniculus? What attendant? My attendant? Surely this fellow is mad.

Messenio. Did I not tell ye what coney-catching villains ye should find here?

Cylindrus. Menaechmus, hark ye sir, ye come too soon back again to dinner; I am but returned from the market.

Menaechmus. Fellow, here thou shalt have money of me. Go, get the priest to sacrifice for thee. I know thou art mad, else thou wouldst never use a stranger thus.

Cylindrus. Alas, sir, Cylindrus was wont to be no stranger to you. Know ye not Cylindrus?

Menaechmus. Cylindrus or Coliendrus or what the devil thou art, I know not, neither do I care to know.

Cylindrus. I know you to be Menaechmus.

Menaechmus. Thou shouldst be in thy wits, in that thou namest me so right; but tell me, where hast thou known me?

Cylindrus. Where? Even here, where ye first fell in love with my mistress, Erotium.

Menaechmus. I neither have lover, neither know I who thou art.

Cylindrus. Know ye not who I am? Who fills your cup and dresses your meat at our house?

Messenio. What a slave is this? That I had somewhat to break the rascal's pate withal!

Menaechmus. At your house, whenas I never came in Epidamnum till this day!

Cylindrus. Oh, that's true. Do ye not dwell in yonder house?

Menaechmus. Foul shame light upon them that dwell there, for my part!

Cylindrus. Questionless, he is mad indeed, to curse himself thus. Hark ye, Menaechmus.

Menaechmus. What sayest thou?

Cylindrus. If I may advise ye, ye shall bestow this money, which ye offered me, upon a sacrifice for yourself; for, out of doubt, you are mad that curse yourself.

Messenio. What a varlet art thou to trouble us thus!

Cylindrus. Tush, he will many times jest with me

thus. Yet when his wife is not by, 'tis a ridiculous jest.

Menaechmus. What's that?

Cylindrus. This I say: think ye I have brought meat enough for three of you? If not, I'll fetch more for you and your wench and Snatchcrust, your parasite.

Menaechmus. What wenches? What parasites?

Messenio. Villain, I'll make thee tell me what thou meanest by all this talk!

Cylindrus. Away, jackanapes! I say nothing to thee, for I know thee not; I speak to him that I know.

Menaechmus. Out, drunken fool! Without doubt thou art out of thy wits.

Cylindrus. That you shall see by the dressing of your meat. Go, go, ye were better to go in and find somewhat to do there, whiles your dinner is making ready. I'll tell my mistress ye be here.

Menaechmus. Is he gone? Messenio, I think upon thy words already.

Messenio. Tush, mark, I pray, I'll lay forty pound here dwells some courtesan to whom this fellow belongs.

Menaechmus. But I wonder how he knows my name.

Messenio. Oh, I'll tell ye. These courtesans, as soon as any strange ship arriveth at the haven, they send a boy or a wench to inquire what they be, what their names be, whence they come, wherefore they come, etcetera. If they can by any means strike acquaintance with him or allure him to their houses, he is their own. We are here in a tickle place, master; 'tis best to be circumspect.

Menaechmus. I mislike not thy counsel, Messenio.

Messenio. Aye, but follow it, then. Soft, here comes somebody forth. Here, sirs, mariners, keep this same among you.

Enter Erotium.

[*Erotium.*] Let the door stand so, away; it shall not be shut. Make haste within there, ho! Maids, look that all things be ready. Cover the board; put fire under the perfuming pans; let all things be very handsome. Where is he, that Cylindrus said stood without here? Oh, what mean you, sweetheart, that ye come not in? I trust you think yourself more welcome to this house than to your own, and great reason why you should do so. Your dinner and all things are ready, as you willed. Will ye go sit down?

Menaechmus. Whom doth this woman speak to?

Erotium. Even to you, sir; to whom else should I speak?

Menaechmus. Gentlewoman, ye are a stranger to me, and I marvel at your speeches.

Erotium. Yea, sir, but such a stranger as I acknowledge ye for my best and dearest friend, and well you have deserved it.

Menaechmus. Surely, Messenio, this woman is also mad or drunk, that useth all this kindness to me upon so small acquaintance.

Messenio. Tush, did I not tell ye right? These be but leaves which fall upon you now, in comparison of trees that will tumble on your neck shortly. I told ye, here were silver-tongued hacksters. But let me talk with her a little. Gentlewoman, what acquaintance have you with this man? Where have you seen him?

Erotium. Where he saw me, here in Epidamnum.

Messenio. In Epidamnum, who never till this day set his foot within the town?

Erotium. Go, go, flouting jack! Menaechmus, what need all this? I pray go in.

Menaechmus. She also calls me by my name.

Messenio. She smells your purse.

Menaechmus. Messenio, come hither, here take my purse. I'll know whether she aim at me or my purse ere I go.

Erotium. Will ye go in to dinner, sir?

Menaechmus. A good notion, yea, and thanks with all my heart.

Erotium. Never thank me for that which you commanded to be provided for yourself.

Menaechmus. That I commanded?

Erotium. Yea, for you and your parasite.

Menaechmus. My parasite?

Erotium. Peniculus, who came with you this morning when you brought me the cloak which you got from your wife.

Menaechmus. A cloak that I brought you, which I got from my wife?

Erotium. Tush, what needeth all this jesting? Pray leave off.

Menaechmus. Jest or earnest, this I tell ye for a truth. I never had wife, neither have I, nor never was in this place till this instant; for only thus far am I come, since I break my fast in the ship.

Erotium. What ship do ye tell me of?

Messenio. Marry, I'll tell ye, an old rotten weather-beaten ship, that we have sailed up and down in this six years. Is't not time to be going homewards, think ye?

Erotium. Come, come, Menaechmus, I pray leave this sporting and go in.

Menaechmus. Well, gentlewoman, the truth is you mistake my person; it is some other that you look for.

Erotium. Why, think ye I know ye not to be Menaechmus, the son of Moschus, and have heard ye say ye were born at Syracuse, where Agathocles did reign, then Phintia, then Liparo, and now Hiero?

Menaechmus. All this is true.

Messenio. Either she is a witch, or else she hath dwelt there and knew ye there.

Menaechmus. I'll go in with her, Messenio; I'll see further of this matter.

Messenio. Ye are cast away, then.

Menaechmus. Why so? I warrant thee, I can lose nothing; somewhat I shall gain, perhaps a good lodging during my abode here. I'll dissemble with her another while. Now, when you please, let us go in; I made strange with you because of this fellow here, lest he should tell my wife of the cloak which I gave you.

Erotium. Will ye stay any longer for your Peniculus, your parasite?

Menaechmus. Not I, I'll neither stay for him nor have him let come in, if he do come.

Erotium. All the better. But sir, will ye do one thing for me?

Menaechmus. What is that?

Erotium. To bear that cloak which you gave me to the dyer's, to have it new trimmed and altered.

Menaechmus. Yea, that will be well, so my wife shall not know it. Let me have it with me after dinner. I will but speak a word or two with this fellow, then I'll follow ye in. Ho, Messenio, come aside. Go and provide for thyself and these ship-boys in some inn; then look that, after dinner, you come hither for me.

Messenio. Ah, master, will ye be coney-catched thus willfully?

Menaechmus. Peace, foolish knave, seest thou not

what a sot she is? I shall cozen her, I warrant thee.

Messenio. Ay, master.

Menaechmus. Wilt thou be gone?

Messenio. See, see, she hath him safe enough now. Thus he hath escaped a hundred pirates' hands at sea, and now one land-rover hath boarded him at first encounter. Come away, fellows.

Act III. Scene I.

Enter Peniculus.

[*Peniculus.*] Twenty years, I think, and more have I played the knave; yet never played I the foolish knave as I have done this morning. I follow Menaechmus, and he goes to the hall where now the sessions are holden. There, thrusting ourselves into the press of people when I was in midst of all the throng, he gave me the slip, that I could never more set eye on him, and, I dare swear, came directly to dinner. That I would he that first devised these sessions were hanged, and all that ever came of him! 'Tis such a hindrance to men that have belly-business in hand. If a man be not there at his call, they amerce him with a vengeance. Men that have nothing else to do, that do neither bid any man nor are themselves bidden to dinner, such should come to sessions; not we that have these matters to look to. If it were so, I had not thus lost my dinner this day; which I think, in my conscience, he did even purposely cozen me of. Yet I mean to go see. If I can but light upon the reversion, I may perhaps get my pennyworth. But how now? Is this Menaechmus coming away from thence, dinner done, and all dispatched? What execrable luck have I!

Enter Menaechmus the Traveler.

[*Menaechmus Traveler.*] Tush, I warrant ye, it shall be done as ye would wish. I'll have it so altered and trimmed anew, that it shall by no means be known again.

Peniculus. He carries the cloak to the dyer's, dinner done, the wine drunk up, the parasite shut out of doors. Well, let me live no longer, but I'll revenge this injurious mockery. But first I'll harken awhile what he saith.

Menaechmus. Good gods, who ever had such luck as I? Such cheer, such a dinner, such kind entertainment! And for a farewell, this cloak, which I mean shall go with me.

Peniculus. He speaks so softly, I cannot hear what he saith; I am sure he is now flouting at me for the loss of my dinner.

Menaechmus. She tells me how I gave it her, and stole it from my wife. When I perceived she was in an error, though I knew not how, I began to soothe her and to say everything as she said. Meanwhile I fared well, and that a-free-cost.

Peniculus. Well, I'll go talk with him.

Menaechmus. Who is this same that comes to me?

Peniculus. O well met, fickle-brain, false and treacherous dealer, crafty and unjust promise-breaker! How have I deserved you should so give me the slip, come before and dispatch the dinner, deal so badly with him that hath reverenced ye like a son?

Menaechmus. Good fellow, what meanest thou by these speeches? Rail not on me, unless thou intendest to receive a railer's hire.

Peniculus. I have received the injury, sure I am already.

Menaechmus. Prithee tell me, what is thy name?

Peniculus. Well, well, mock on, sir, mock on; do ye not know my name?

Menaechmus. In troth, I never saw thee in all my life, much less do I know thee.

Peniculus. Fie, awake, Menaechmus, awake, ye oversleep yourself.

Menaechmus. I am awake; I know what I say.

Peniculus. Know you not Peniculus?

Menaechmus. Peniculus or Pediculus, I know thee not.

Peniculus. Did ye filch a cloak from your wife this morning and bring it hither to Erotium?

Menaechmus. Neither have I wife, neither gave I any cloak to Erotium, neither filched I any from anybody.

Peniculus. Will ye deny that which you did in my company?

Menaechmus. Wilt thou say I have done this in thy company?

Peniculus. Will I say it? Yea, I will stand to it.

Menaechmus. Away, filthy mad drivel, away! I will talk no longer with thee.

Peniculus. Not a world of men shall stay me, but I'll go tell his wife of all the whole matter, sith he is at this point with me. I will make this same as unblest a dinner as ever he eat.

Menaechmus. It makes me wonder to see how everyone that meets me cavils thus with me. Wherefore comes forth the maid now?

Enter Ancilla, Erotium's maid.

Ancilla. Menaechmus, my mistress commends her heartily to you; and, seeing you go that way to the dyer's, she also desireth you to take this chain with you and put it to mending at the goldsmith's; she would have two or three ounces of gold more in it, and the fashion amended.

Menaechmus. Either this or anything else within my power, tell her, I am ready to accomplish.

Ancilla. Do ye know this chain, sir?

Menaechmus. Yea, I know it to be gold.

Ancilla. This is the same you once took out of your wife's casket.

Menaechmus. Who, did I?

Ancilla. Have you forgotten?

Menaechmus. I never did it.

Ancilla. Give it me again, then.

Menaechmus. Tarry; yes, I remember it; 'tis it I gave your mistress.

Ancilla. Oh, are ye advised?

Menaechmus. Where are the bracelets that I gave her likewise?

Ancilla. I never knew of any.

Menaechmus. Faith, when I gave this, I gave them too.

Ancilla. Well, sir, I'll tell her this shall be done?

Menaechmus. Ay, ay, tell her so; she shall have the cloak and this both together.

Ancilla. I pray, Menaechmus, put a little jewel for my ear to making for me; ye know I am always ready to pleasure you.

Menaechmus. I will. Give me the gold; I'll pay for the workmanship.

Ancilla. Lay out for me; I'll pay it ye again.

Menaechmus. Alas, I have none now.

Ancilla. When you have, will ye?

Menaechmus. I will. Go bid your mistress make no
doubt of these; I warrant her, I'll make the best
hand I can of them. Is she gone? Do not all the
gods conspire to load me with good luck? Well, I
see 'tis high time to get me out of these coats, lest
all these matters should be lewd devices to draw
me into some snare. There shall my garland lie,
because if they seek me, they may think I am gone
that way. I will now go see if I can find my man
Messenio, that I may tell him how I have sped.

Act IV. Scene I.

*Enter Mulier, the Wife of Menaechmus the Citizen,
and Peniculus.*

Mulier. Thinks he I will be made such a sot, and to
be still his drudge, while he prowls and purloins all
that I have to give his trulls?

Peniculus. Nay, hold your peace; we'll catch him in
the nick. This way he came, in his garland forsooth,
bearing the cloak to the dyer's. And see, I pray,
where the garland lies; this way he is gone. See, see,
where he comes again now without the cloak.

Mulier. What shall I now do?

Peniculus. What? That which ye ever do, bait him for
life.

Mulier. Surely I think it best so.

Peniculus. Stay, we will stand aside a little; ye shall
catch him unawares.

Enter Menaechmus the Citizen.

Menaechmus. It would make a man at his wit's end
to see how brabbling causes are handled yonder at
the court. If a poor man, never so honest, have a

matter come to be scanned, there is he outfaced
and overlaid with countenance. If a rich man, never
so vile a wretch, come to speak, there they are all
ready to favor his cause. What with facing out bad
causes for the oppressors and patronizing some
just actions for the wronged, the lawyers they
pocket up all the gains. For mine own part, I come
not away empty, though I have been kept long
against my will. For taking in hand to dispatch a
matter this morning for one of my acquaintance, I
was no sooner entered into it, but his adversaries
laid so hard unto his charge and brought such
matter against him that, do what I could, I could
not wind myself out till now. I am sore afraid
Erotium thinks much unkindness in me that I stayed
so long; yet she will not be angry, considering the
gift I gave her today.

Peniculus. How think ye by that?

Mulier. I think him a most vile wretch thus to abuse
me.

Menaechmus. I will hie me thither.

Mulier. Yea, go, pilferer, go with shame enough; nobody sees your lewd dealings and vile thievery.

Menaechmus. How now, wife, what ail ye? What is
the matter?

Mulier. Ask ye me what's the matter? Fie upon thee!

Peniculus. Are ye not in a fit of an ague, your pulses
beat so sore? To him, I say!

Menaechmus. Pray, wife, why are ye so angry with
me?

Mulier. Oh, you know not?

Peniculus. He knows, but he would dissemble it.

Menaechmus. What is it?

Mulier. My cloak.

Menaechmus. Your cloak?

Mulier. My cloak, man, why do ye blush?

Peniculus. He cannot cloak his blushing. Nay, I might not go to dinner with you, do ye remember? To him, I say!

Menaechmus. Hold thy peace, Peniculus.

Peniculus. Ha, hold my peace! Look ye, he beckons on me to hold my peace.

Menaechmus. I neither beckon nor wink on him.

Mulier. Out, out, what a wretched life is this that I live!

Menaechmus. Why, what ail ye, woman?

Mulier. Are ye not ashamed to deny so confidently that which is apparent?

Menaechmus. I protest unto you before all the gods— is not this enough?—that I beckoned not on him.

Peniculus. Oh, sir, this is another matter; touch him in the former cause.

Menaechmus. What former cause?

Peniculus. The cloak, man, the cloak; fetch the cloak again from the dyer's.

Menaechmus. What cloak?

Mulier. Nay, I'll say no more, with ye know nothing of your own doings.

Menaechmus. Tell me, wife, hath any of your servants abused you? Let me know.

Mulier. Tush, tush!

Menaechmus. I would not have you to be thus disquieted.

Mulier. Tush, tush!

Menaechmus. You are fallen out with some of your friends.

Mulier. Tush, tush!

Menaechmus. Sure I am I have not offended you.

Mulier. No, you have dealt very honestly.

Menaechmus. Indeed, wife, I have deserved none of these words. Tell me, are ye not well?

Peniculus. What, shall he flatter ye now?

Menaechmus. I speak not to thee, knave. Good wife, come hither.

Mulier. Away, away, keep your hands off!

Peniculus. So, bid me to dinner with you again; then slip away from me; when you have done, come forth bravely in your garland to flout me. Alas, you knew not me even now.

Menaechmus. Why, ass, I neither have yet dined, nor came I there since we were there together.

Peniculus. Who ever heard one so impudent? Did ye not meet me here even now, and would make me believe I was mad, and said ye were a stranger and ye knew me not?

Menaechmus. Of a truth, since we went together to the sessions hall, I never returned till this very instant as you two met me.

Peniculus. Go to, go to, I know ye well enough. Did ye think I would not cry quittance with you? Yes, faith, I have told your wife all.

Menaechmus. What hast thou told her?

Peniculus. I cannot tell, ask her.

Menaechmus. Tell me, wife, what hath he told ye of me? Tell me, I say, what was it?

Mulier. As though you knew not! My cloak is stolen from me.

Menaechmus. Is your cloak stolen from ye?

Mulier. Do ye ask me?

Menaechmus. If I knew, I would not ask.

Peniculus. O crafty companion, how he would shift the matter! Come, come, deny it not; I tell ye, I have bewrayed all.

Menaechmus. What hast thou bewrayed?

Mulier. Seeing ye will yield to nothing be it never so manifest. Hear me, and ye shall know in few words both the cause of my grief and what he hath told me. I say, my cloak is stolen from me.

Menaechmus. My cloak is stolen from me?

Peniculus. Look how he cavils; she saith it is stolen from her.

Menaechmus. I have nothing to say to thee. I say, wife, tell me.

Mulier. I tell ye, my cloak is stolen out of my house.

Menaechmus. Who stole it?

Mulier. He knows best that carried it away.

Menaechmus. Who was that?

Mulier. Menaechmus.

Menaechmus. 'Twas very ill done of him. What Menaechmus was that?

Mulier. You.

Menaechmus. I? Who will say so?

Mulier. I will.

Peniculus. And I; and that you gave it to Erotium.

Menaechmus. I gave it?

Mulier. You.

Peniculus. You, you, you! Shall we fetch a kennel of beagles that may cry nothing but "you," "you," "you," "you"? For we are weary of it.

Menaechmus. Hear me one word, wife. I protest unto you by all the gods, I gave it her not; indeed, I lent it her to use a while.

Mulier. Faith, sir, I never give nor lend you apparel out of doors; methinks ye might let me dispose of mine own garments, as you do of yours. I pray then fetch it me home again.

Menaechmus. You shall have it again without fail.

Mulier. 'Tis best for you that I have; otherwise think not to roost within these doors again.

Peniculus. Hark ye, what say ye to me now for bringing these matters to your knowledge?

Mulier. I say when thou hast anything stolen from thee, come to me and I will help thee to seek it. And so farewell.

Peniculus. God-a-mercy for nothing, that can never be; for I have nothing in the world worth the stealing. So now with husband and wife and all, I am clean out of favor. A mischief on ye all!   *Exit.*

Menaechmus. My wife thinks she is notably revenged on me, now she shuts me out of doors, as though I had not a better place to be welcome to. If she shut me out, I know who will shut me in. Now will I entreat Erotium to let me have the cloak again to stop my wife's mouth withal, and then will I provide a better for her. Ho, who is within there? Somebody tell Erotium I must speak with her.

Enter Erotium.

Erotium. Who calls?

Menaechmus. Your friend, more than his own.

Erotium. O Menaechmus, why stand ye here? Pray come in.

Menaechmus. Tarry, I must speak with ye here.

Erotium. Say your mind.

Menaechmus. Wot ye what? My wife knows all the matter now, and my coming is to request you that I may have again the cloak which I brought you, that so I may appease her; and I promise you, I'll give you another worth two of it.

Erotium. Why, I gave it you to carry to your dyer's and my chain likewise, to have it altered.

Menaechmus. Gave me the cloak and your chain? In truth, I never saw ye since I left it here with you and so went to the sessions, from whence I am but now returned.

Erotium. Ah, then, sir, I see you wrought a device to defraud me of them both. Did I therefore put ye in trust? Well, well!

Menaechmus. To defraud ye? No, but I say my wife hath intelligence of the matter.

Erotium. Why, sir, I asked them not; ye brought them me of your own free motion. Now ye require them again, take them, make fops of them. You and your wife together, think ye I esteem them or you either? Go, come to me again when I send for you.

Menaechmus. What, so angry with me, sweet Erotium? Stay, I pray, stay.

Erotium. Stay? Faith, sir, no. Think ye I will stay at your request?

Menaechmus. What, gone in chafing, and clapped to the doors? Now I am every way shut out for a very bench-whistler; neither shall I have entertainment here nor at home. I were best go try some other friends, and ask counsel what to do.

Act V. Scene I.

Enter Menaechmus the Traveler, Mulier.

[*Menaechmus Traveler.*] Most foolishly was I over-seen in giving my purse and money to Messenio, whom I can nowhere find. I fear he is fallen into some lewd company.

Mulier. I marvel that my husband comes not yet. But see where he is now, and brings my cloak with him.

Menaechmus. I muse where the knave should be.

Mulier. I will go ring a peal through both his ears for this his dishonest behavior. Oh, sir, ye are welcome home with your thievery on your shoulders. Are ye not ashamed to let all the world see and speak of your lewdness?

Menaechmus. How now? What lacks this woman?

Mulier. Impudent beast, stand ye to question about it? For shame, hold thy peace.

Menaechmus. What offense have I done, woman, that I should not speak to you?

Mulier. Asketh thou what offense? O shameless boldness!

Menaechmus. Good woman, did ye never hear why the Grecians termed Hecuba to be a bitch?

Mulier. Never.

Menaechmus. Because she did as you do now: on whomsoever she met withal she railed, and therefore well deserved that dogged name.

Mulier. These foul abuses and contumelies I can never endure; nay, rather will I live a widow's life to my dying day.

Menaechmus. What care I whether thou livest as a widow or as a wife? This passeth, that I meet with none but thus they vex me with strange speeches.

Mulier. What strange speeches? I say I will surely live a widow's life rather than suffer thy vile dealings.

Menaechmus. Prithee, for my part, live a widow till the world's end, if thou wilt.

Mulier. Even now thou deniedst that thou stolest it

from me, and now thou bringest it home openly in my sight. Art not ashamed?

Menaechmus. Woman, you are greatly to blame to charge me with stealing of this cloak, which this day another gave me to carry to be trimmed.

Mulier. Well, I will first complain to my father. Ho, boy, who is within there? Decio, go run quickly to my father; desire him of all love to come over quickly to my house. I'll tell him first of your pranks. I hope he will not see me thus handled.

Menaechmus. What, a God's name, meaneth this madwoman thus to vex me?

Mulier. I am mad because I tell ye of your vile actions and lewd pilfering away of my apparel and my jewels to carry to your filthy drabs.

Menaechmus. For whom this woman taketh me I know not; I know her as much as I know Hercules' wife's father.

Mulier. Do ye not know me? That's well, I hope ye know my father. Here he comes. Look, do ye know him?

Menaechmus. As much as I knew Calchas of Troy. Even him and thee I know both alike.

Mulier. Dost know neither of us both, me nor my father?

Menaechmus. Faith, nor thy grandfather neither.

Mulier. This is like the rest of your behavior.

Enter Senex.

[*Senex.*] Though bearing so great a burden as old age, I can make no great haste; yet as I can I will go to my daughter, who I know hath some earnest business with me, that she sends in such haste, not telling the cause why I should come. But I durst lay a wager, I can guess near the matter: I suppose it is some brabble between her husband and her.

These young women that bring great dowries to
their husbands are so masterful and obstinate that
they will have their own wills in everything, and
make men servants to their weak affections. And
young men too, I must needs say, be naught now-
adays. Well I'll go see; but yonder, methinks,
stands my daughter and her husband too. Oh, 'tis
even as I guessed.

Mulier. Father, ye are welcome.

Senex. How now, daughter? What, is all well? Why
is your husband so sad? Have ye been chiding?
Tell me, which of you is in the fault?

Mulier. First, father, know that I have not any way
misbehaved myself; but the truth is, I can by no
means endure this bad man, to die for it; and therefore desire you to take me home to you again.

Senex. What is the matter?

Mulier. He makes me a stale and a laughingstock to
all the world.

Senex. Who doth?

Mulier. This good husband here, to whom you married me.

Senex. See, see, how oft have I warned you of falling
out with your husband!

Mulier. I cannot avoid it, if he doth so foully abuse
me.

Senex. I always told ye, you must bear with him; ye
must let him alone; ye must not watch him nor dog
him nor meddle with his courses in any sort.

Mulier. He haunts naughty harlots under my nose.

Senex. He is the wiser, because he cannot be quiet at
home.

Mulier. There he feasts and banquets, and spends and
spoils.

Senex. Would ye have your husband serve ye as your

drudge? Ye will not let him make merry nor entertain his friends at home.

Mulier. Father, will ye take his part in these abuses, and forsake me?

Senex. Not so, daughter; but if I see cause, I will as well tell him of his duty.

Menaechmus. I would I were gone from this prating father and daughter.

Senex. Hitherto I see not but he keeps ye well; ye want nothing, apparel, money, servants, meat, drink, all things necessary. I fear there is fault in you.

Mulier. But he filcheth away my apparel and my jewels to give to his trulls.

Senex. If he doth so, 'tis very ill done; if not, you do ill to say so.

Mulier. You may believe me, father; for there you may see my cloak which now he hath fetched home again, and my chain which he stole from me.

Senex. Now will I go talk with him to know the truth. Tell me, Menaechmus, how is it that I hear such disorder in your life? Why are ye so sad, man? Wherein hath your wife offended you?

Menaechmus. Old man—what to call ye I know not— by high Jove and by all the gods I swear unto you, whatsoever this woman here accuseth me to have stolen from her, it is utterly false and untrue; and if I ever set foot within her doors, I wish the greatest misery in the world to light upon me.

Senex. Why, fond man, art thou mad to deny that thou ever setst foot within thine own house where thou dwellest?

Menaechmus. Do I dwell in that house?

Senex. Dost thou deny it?

Menaechmus. I do.

Senex. Hark ye, daughter, are ye removed out of your house?

Mulier. Father, he useth you as he doth me, this life I have with him.

Senex. Menaechmus, I pray leave this fondness; ye jest too perversely with your friends.

Menaechmus. Good old father, what, I pray, have you to do with me? Or why should this woman thus trouble me, with whom I have no dealings in the world?

Mulier. Father, mark, I pray, how his eyes sparkle! They roll in his head; his color goes and comes; he looks wildly. See, see!

Menaechmus. What! they say now I am mad; the best way for me is to feign myself mad indeed, so I shall be rid of them.

Mulier. Look how he stares about! Now he gapes.

Senex. Come away, daughter, come from him.

Menaechmus. Bacchus, Apollo, Phoebus, do ye call me to come hunt in the woods with you? I see, I hear, I come, I fly, but I cannot get out of these fields. Here is an old mastiff bitch stands barking at me, and by her stands an old goat that bears false witness against many a poor man.

Senex. Out upon him, Bedlam fool!

Menaechmus. Hark, Apollo commands me that I should rend out her eyes with a burning lamp!

Mulier. O father, he threatens to pull out mine eyes!

Menaechmus. Good gods, these folk say I am mad, and doubtless they are mad themselves.

Senex. Daughter!

Mulier. Here, father, what shall we do?

Senex. What if I fetch my folks hither, and have him carried in before he do any harm?

Menaechmus. How now! They will carry me in, if I look not to myself. I were best to scare them better yet. Dost thou bid me, Phoebus, to tear this dog in pieces with my nails? If I lay hold on him, I will do thy commandment.

Senex. Get thee into thy house, daughter; away quickly!

Menaechmus. She is gone. Yea, Apollo, I will sacrifice this old beast unto thee; and if thou commandest me, I will cut his throat with that dagger that hangs at his girdle.

Senex. Come not near me, sirrah!

Menaechmus. Yea, I will quarter him, and pull all the bones out of his flesh; then will I barrel up his bowels.

Senex. Sure, I am sore afraid he will do some hurt.

Menaechmus. Many things thou commandest me, Apollo. Wouldst thou have me harness up these wild horses, and then climb up into the chariot, and so override this old stinking toothless lion? So now I am in the chariot, and I have hold on the reins; here is my whip. Hait! Come ye wild jades, make a hideous noise with your stamping; hait, I say, will ye not go?

Senex. What! Doth he threaten me with his horses?

Menaechmus. Hark, now Apollo bids me ride over him that stands there and kill him. How now? Who pulls me down from my chariot by the hairs of my head? Oh, shall I not fulfill Apollo's commandment?

Senex. See, see, what a sharp disease this is, and how well he was even now! I will fetch a physician straight, before he grow too far into this rage. *Exit.*

Menaechmus. Are they both gone now? I'll then hie me away to my ship; 'tis time to be gone from hence. *Exit.*

Enter Senex and Medicus.

Senex. My loins ache with sitting, and mine eyes with looking, while I stay for yonder lazy physician. See now where the creeping draw-latch comes.

Medicus. What disease hath he said you? Is it a lethargy or a lunacy or melancholy or dropsy?

Senex. Wherefore, I pray, do I bring you but that you should tell me what it is, and cure him of it?

Medicus. Fie, make no question of that; I'll cure him, I warrant ye. Oh, here he comes; stay, let us mark what he doth.

Enter Menaechmus the Citizen.

Menaechmus. Never in my life had I more overthwart fortune in one day, and all by the villainy of this false knave, the parasite, my Ulysses that works such mischiefs against me, his king. But let me live no longer, but I'll be revenged upon the life of him. His life? Nay, 'tis my life; for he lives by my meat and drink. I'll utterly withdraw the slave's life from him. And Erotium she showeth plainly what she is, who, because I require the cloak again to carry to my wife, saith I gave it her and flatly falls out with me. How unfortunate am I!

Senex. Do ye hear him?

Medicus. He complains of his fortune.

Senex. Go to him.

Medicus. Menaechmus, how do ye, man? Why keep you not your cloak over your arm? It is very hurtful to your disease. Keep ye warm, I pray.

Menaechmus. Why, hang thyself, what carest thou?

Medicus. Sir, can you smell anything?

Menaechmus. I smell a prating dolt of thee.

Medicus. Oh, I will have your head throughly purged. Pray tell me, Menaechmus, what use you to drink? White wine or claret?

Menaechmus. What the devil carest thou?

Senex. Look, his fit now begins.

Menaechmus. Why dost not as well ask me whether I eat bread, or cheese, or beef, or porridge, or birds that bear feathers, or fishes that have fins?

Senex. See, what idle talk he falleth into!

Medicus. Tarry, I will ask him further. Menaechmus, tell me, be not your eyes heavy and dull sometimes?

Menaechmus. What dost think I am, an owl?

Medicus. Do not your guts gripe ye and croak in your belly?

Menaechmus. When I am hungry they do, else not.

Medicus. He speaks not like a madman in that. Sleep ye soundly all night?

Menaechmus. When I have paid my debts I do. The mischief light on thee, with all thy frivolous questions!

Medicus. Oh, now he rageth upon those words; take heed.

Senex. Oh, this is nothing to the rage he was in even now. He called his wife bitch, and all to naught.

Menaechmus. Did I?

Senex. Thou didst, mad fellow, and threatened to ride over me here with a chariot and horses, and to kill me, and tear me in pieces. This thou didst; I know what I say.

Menaechmus. I say thou stolest Jupiter's crown from his head and thou wert whipped through the town for it, and that thou hast killed thy father and beaten thy mother. Do ye think I am so mad that I cannot devise as notable lies of you as you do of me?

Senex. Master doctor, pray heartily make speed to cure him; see ye not how mad he waxeth?

Medicus. I'll tell ye, he shall be brought over to my house, and there will I cure him.

Senex. Is that best?

Medicus. What else? There I can order him as I list.

Senex. Well, it shall be so.

Medicus. Oh sir, I will make ye take [s]neezing powder this twenty days.

Menaechmus. I'll beat ye first with a bastinado this thirty days.

Medicus. Fetch men to carry him to my house.

Senex. How many will serve the turn?

Medicus. Being no madder than he is now, four will serve.

Senex. I'll fetch them. Stay you with him, master doctor.

Medicus. No, by my faith, I'll go home to make ready all things needful. Let your men bring him thither.

Senex. I go.   *Exeunt.*

Menaechmus. Are they both gone? Good gods, what meaneth this? These men say I am mad, who without doubt are mad themselves. I stir not, I fight not, I am not sick. I speak to them, I know them. Well, what were I now best to do? I would go home, but my wife shuts me forth a-doors. Erotium is as far out with me too. Even here I will rest me till the evening; I hope by that time they will take pity on me.

Enter Messenio, the Traveler's servant.

[*Messenio.*] The proof of a good servant is to regard his master's business as well in his absence as in his presence; and I think him a very fool that is not careful as well for his ribs and shoulders as for his belly and throat. When I think upon the rewards of a sluggard, I am ever pricked with a careful regard of my back and shoulders; for, in truth, I have no fancy to these blows, as many a one hath. Methinks it is no pleasure to a man to be basted with a rope's end two or three hours together. I have provided yonder in the town for all our mariners, and safely bestowed all my master's trunks and fardels; and am now coming to see if he be yet got forth of this dangerous gulf, where I fear me [he] is over-plunged—pray God he be not overwhelmed and past help ere I come!

Enter Senex, with four Lorarii [porters].

[*Senex.*] Before gods and men, I charge and command you, sirs, to execute with great care that which I appoint you. If ye love the safety of your own ribs and shoulders, then go take me up my son-in-law, lay all hands upon him. Why stand ye still? What do ye doubt? I say, care not for his threatenings, nor for any of his words. Take him up and bring him to the physician's house. I will go thither before. *Exit.*

Menaechmus. What news? How now, masters! What will ye do with me? Why do ye thus beset me? Whither carry ye me? Help, help, neighbors, friends, citizens!

Messenio. O Jupiter, what do I see? My master abused by a company of varlets.

Menaechmus. Is there no good man will help me?

Messenio. Help ye, master? Yes, the villains shall have my life before they shall thus wrong ye. 'Tis more fit I should be killed than you thus handled. Pull out that rascal's eye that holds ye about the neck there! I'll clout these peasants. Out, ye rogue! Let go, ye varlet!

Menaechmus. I have hold of this villain's eye.

Messenio. Pull it out and let the place appear in his head! Away, ye cutthroat thieves, ye murderers!

Lorarii Omnes. O, o! Aye, aye! *Cry pitifully.*

Messenio. Away, get ye hence, ye mongrels, ye dogs! Will ye be gone? Thou rascal behind there, I'll give thee somewhat more; take that! It was time to come, master; you had been in good case if I had not been here now! I told you what would come of it.

Menaechmus. Now, as the gods love me, my good friend, I thank thee. Thou hast done that for me which I shall never be able to requite.

Messenio. I'll tell ye how, sir: give me my freedom.

Menaechmus. Should I give it thee?

Messenio. Seeing you cannot requite my good turn.

Menaechmus. Thou art deceived, man.

Messenio. Wherein?

Menaechmus. On mine honesty, I am none of thy master; I had never yet any servant would do so much for me.

Messenio. Why, then bid me be free; will you?

Menaechmus. Yea surely, be free, for my part.

Messenio. O sweetly spoken! Thanks, my good master.

Servus alius. Messenio, we are all glad of your good fortune.

Messenio. O master, I'll call ye master still; I pray, use me in any service as ye did before; I'll dwell with you still, and when ye go home I'll wait upon you.

Menaechmus. Nay, nay, it shall not need.

Messenio. I'll go straight to the inn and deliver up my accounts and all your stuff. Your purse is locked up safely sealed in the casket, as you gave it me. I will go fetch it to you.

Menaechmus. Do, fetch it.

Messenio. I will.

Menaechmus. I was never thus perplexed. Some deny
me to be him that I am and shut me out of their
doors. This fellow saith he is my bondman, and of
me he begs his freedom. He will fetch my purse
and money. Well, if he bring it, I will receive it,
and let him free. I would he would so go his way.
My old father-in-law and the doctor say I am mad.
Who ever saw such strange demeanors? Well,
though Erotium be never so angry, yet once again
I'll go see if by entreaty I can get the cloak on her
to carry to my wife.   *Exit.*

Enter Menaechmus the Traveler and Messenio.

Menaechmus. Impudent knave, wilt thou say that I
ever saw thee since I sent thee away today and bade
thee come for me after dinner?

Messenio. Ye make me stark mad. I took ye away and
rescued ye from four great big-boned villains, that
were carrying ye away even here in this place. Here
they had ye up; and cried, "Help, help!" I came
running to you; you and I together beat them away
by main force. Then, for thy good turn and faithful service, ye gave me my freedom. I told ye I
would go fetch your casket; now, in the mean time,
you ran some other way to get before me; and so
you deny it all again.

Menaechmus. I gave thee thy freedom?

Messenio. You did.

Menaechmus. When I give thee thy freedom, I'll be
a bondman myself. Go thy ways.

Enter Menaechmus the Citizen.

[*Menaechmus Citizen.*] Forsworn queans, swear till
your hearts ache and your eyes fall out, ye shall
never make me believe that I carried hence either
cloak or chain.

Messenio. O heavens, master, what do I see?

Menaechmus Traveler. What?

Messenio. Your ghost.

Menaechmus Traveler. What ghost?

Messenio. Your image, as like you as can be possible.

Menaechmus Traveler. Surely not much unlike me as I think.

Menaechmus Citizen. O my good friend and helper, well me! Thanks for thy late good help.

Messenio. Sir, may I crave to know your name?

Menaechmus Citizen. I were to blame if I should not tell thee anything; my name is Menaechmus.

Menaechmus Traveler. Nay, my friend, that is my name.

Menaechmus Citizen. I am of Syracuse in Sicilia.

Menaechmus Traveler. So am I.

Messenio. Are you a Syracusan?

Menaechmus Citizen. I am.

Messenio. O ho, I know ye! This is my master; I thought he there had been my master, and was proffering my service to him; pray pardon me, sir, if I said anything I should not.

Menaechmus Traveler. Why, doting patch, didst thou not come with me this morning from the ship?

Messenio. My faith, he says true, this is my master; you may go look ye a man. God save ye, master. You, sir, farewell. This is Menaechmus.

Menaechmus Citizen. I say that I am Menaechmus.

Messenio. What a jest is this? Are you Menaechmus?

Menaechmus Citizen. Even Menaechmus, the son of Moschus.

Menaechmus Traveler. My father's son?

Menaechmus Citizen. Friend, I go about neither to take your father nor your country from you.

Messenio. O immortal gods, let it fall out as I hope, and for my life these are two twins; all things agree so jump together. I will speak to my master. Menaechmus?

Both. What wilt thou?

Messenio. I call ye not both; but which of you came with me from the ship?

Menaechmus Citizen. Not I.

Menaechmus Traveler. I did.

Messenio. Then I call you. Come hither.

Menaechmus Traveler. What's the matter?

Messenio. This same is either some notable cozening juggler or else it is your brother whom we seek. I never saw one man so like another; water to water, nor milk to milk, is not liker than he is to you.

Menaechmus Traveler. Indeed, I think thou sayest true. Find it that he is my brother, and I here promise thee thy freedom.

Messenio. Well, let me about it. Hear ye, sir, ye say your name is Menaechmus?

Menaechmus Citizen. I do.

Messenio. So is this man's. You are of Syracuse?

Menaechmus Citizen. True.

Messenio. So is he. Moschus was your father?

Menaechmus Citizen. He was.

Messenio. So was his. What will you say if I find that ye are brethren and twins?

Menaechmus Citizen. I would think it happy news.

Messenio. Nay, stay, masters both, I mean to have the honor of this exploit. Answer me: your name is Menaechmus?

Menaechmus Citizen. Yea.

Messenio. And yours?

Menaechmus Traveler. And mine.

Messenio. You are of Syracuse?

Menaechmus Citizen. I am.

Menaechmus Traveler. And I.

Messenio. Well, this goeth right thus far. What is the farthest thing that you remember there?

Menaechmus Citizen. How I went with my father to Tarentum, to a great mart, and there in the press I was stolen from him.

Menaechmus Traveler. O Jupiter!

Messenio. Peace, what exclaiming is this? How old were ye then?

Menaechmus Citizen. About seven year old; for even then I shed teeth; and since that time, I never heard of any of my kindred.

Messenio. Had ye never a brother?

Menaechmus Citizen. Yes, as I remember, I heard them say we were two twins.

Menaechmus Traveler. O fortune!

Messenio. Tush, can ye not be quiet? Were ye both of one name?

Menaechmus Citizen. Nay, as I think, they called my brother Sosicles.

Menaechmus Traveler. It is he; what need farther proof? O brother, brother, let me embrace thee!

Menaechmus Citizen. Sir, if this be true, I am wonderfully glad; but how is it, that ye are called Menaechmus?

Menaechmus Traveler. When it was told us that you and our father were both dead, our grandsire, in memory of my father's name, changed mine to Menaechmus.

Menaechmus Citizen. 'Tis very like he would do so, indeed. But let me ask ye one question more: what was our mother's name?

Menaechmus Traveler. Teuximarcha.

Menaechmus Citizen. Brother, the most welcome man to me, that the world holdeth.

Menaechmus Traveler. I joy, and ten thousand joys the more, having taken so long travail and huge pains to seek you.

Messenio. See now, how all this matter comes about. This it was, that the gentlewoman had ye in to dinner, thinking it had been he.

Menaechmus Citizen. True it is. I willed a dinner to be provided for me here this morning, and I also brought hither closely a cloak of my wife's, and gave it to this woman.

Menaechmus Traveler. Is not this the same, brother?

Menaechmus Citizen. How came you by this?

Menaechmus Traveler. This woman met me, had me in to dinner, entertained me most kindly, and gave me this cloak and this chain.

Menaechmus Citizen. Indeed, she took ye for me; and I believe I have been as strangely handled by occasion of your coming.

Messenio. You shall have time enough to laugh at all these matters hereafter. Do ye remember, master, what ye promised me?

Menaechmus Citizen. Brother, I will entreat you to perform your promise to Messenio; he is worthy of it.

Menaechmus Traveler. I am content.

Messenio. "Io triumphe!"

Menaechmus Traveler. Brother, will ye now go with me to Syracuse?

Menaechmus Citizen. So soon as I can sell away such goods as I possess here in Epidamnum, I will go with you.

Menaechmus Traveler. Thanks, my good brother.

Menaechmus Citizen. Messenio, play thou the crier for me, and make a proclamation.

Messenio. A fit office. Come on. Oyez! What day shall your sale be?

Menaechmus Citizen. This day se'nnight.

Messenio. All men, women, and children in Epidamnum or elsewhere that will repair to Menaechmus' house this day se'nnight shall there find all manner of things to sell: servants, household stuff, house, ground, and all, so they bring ready money. Will ye sell your wife too, sir?

Menaechmus Citizen. Yea, but I think nobody will bid money for her.

Messenio. Thus, gentlemen, we take our leaves; and if we have pleased, we require a *plaudite*.

FINIS

Commentaries

AUGUST WILHELM SCHLEGEL

from *Lectures on Dramatic Art and Literature*

The Comedy of Errors is the subject of the *Menaechmi* of Plautus, entirely recast and enriched with new developments: of all the works of Shakespeare this is the only example of imitation of, or borrowing from, the ancients. To the two twin brothers of the same name are added two slaves, also twins, impossible to be distinguished from each other, and of the same name. The improbability becomes by this means doubled: but when once we have lent ourselves to the first, which certainly borders on the incredible, we shall not perhaps be disposed to cavil at the second; and if the spectator is to be entertained by mere perplexities they cannot be too varied. In such pieces we must, to give the senses at least an appearance of truth, always presuppose that the parts by which the misunderstandings are occasioned are played with masks, and this the poet no doubt observed. I cannot acquiesce in the censure that the discovery is too long deferred: so long as novelty and interest are possessed by the perplexing incidents there is no need to be in dread of wearisomeness. And this is really the case here: matters are

From *Lectures on Dramatic Art and Literature* by August Wilhelm Schlegel, translated by John Black. London: George Bell & Sons, 1889. Schlegel's lectures, delivered at Vienna in 1808, and amplified in the German text of 1811, were translated by Black in 1815. The translation underwent slight revision in subsequent printings.

carried so far that one of the two brothers is first arrested
for debt, then confined as a lunatic, and the other is forced
to take refuge in a sanctuary to save his life. In a subject
of this description it is impossible to steer clear of all sorts
of low circumstances, abusive language, and blows; Shakespeare has however endeavored to ennoble it in every
possible way. A couple of scenes, dedicated to jealousy
and love, interrupt the course of perplexities which are
solely occasioned by the illusion of the external senses. A
greater solemnity is given to the discovery, from the
Prince presiding, and from the reunion of the long-sepa-
rated parents of the twins who are still alive. The exposi-
tion, by which the spectators are previously instructed
while the characters themselves are still involved in ignorance, and which Plautus artlessly conveys in a prologue, is here masterly introduced in an affecting narrative
by the father. In short, this is perhaps the best of all written or possible *Menaechmi;* and if the piece be inferior
in worth to other pieces of Shakespeare, it is merely because nothing more could be made of the materials.

SAMUEL TAYLOR COLERIDGE

from *Shakespearean Criticism*

The myriad-minded man, our, and all men's, Shak-
speare, has in this piece presented us with a legitimate
farce in exactest consonance with the philosophical prin-
ciples and character of farce, as distinguished from comedy and from entertainments. A proper farce is mainly

From *Shakespearean Criticism* by Samuel Taylor Coleridge. 2nd ed.,
edited by Thomas Middleton Raysor. 2 vols. New York: E. P. Dutton and
Company, Inc., 1960; London: J. M. Dent & Sons, Ltd., 1961.

distinguished from comedy by the license allowed, and
even required, in the fable, in order to produce strange
and laughable situations. The story need not be probable,
it is enough that it is possible. A comedy would scarcely
allow even the two Antipholuses; because, although there
have been instances of almost indistinguishable likeness in
two persons, yet these are mere individual accidents, *casus
ludentis naturae,* and the *verum* will not excuse the *in-
verisimile.* But farce dares add the two Dromios, and is
justified in so doing by the laws of its end and constitu-
tion. In a word, farces commence in a postulate, which
must be granted.

*   *   *

. . . remarkable as being the only specimen of *poetical
farce* in our language, that is, intentionally such. . . .

WILLIAM HAZLITT

from *Characters of Shakespear's Plays*

This comedy is taken very much from the *Menaechmi*
of Plautus, and is not an improvement on it. Shakespear
appears to have bestowed no great pains on it, and there
are but a few passages which bear the decided stamp of
his genius. He seems to have relied on his author, and on
the interest arising out of the intricacy of the plot. The
curiosity excited is certainly very considerable, though not
of the most pleasing kind. We are teased as with a riddle,
which notwithstanding we try to solve. In reading the play,
from the sameness of the names of the two Antipholuses
and the two Dromios, as well from their being constantly

From *Characters of Shakespear's Plays* by William Hazlitt. 2nd ed.
London: Taylor & Hessey, 1818.

taken for each other by those who see them, it is difficult, without a painful effort of attention, to keep the characters distinct in the mind. And again, on the stage, either the complete similarity of their persons and dress must produce the same perplexity whenever they first enter, or the identity of appearance which the story supposes, will be destroyed. We still, however, having a clue to the difficulty, can tell which is which, merely from the practical contradictions which arise, as soon as the different parties begin to speak; and we are indemnified for the perplexity and blunders into which we are thrown by seeing others thrown into greater and almost inextricable ones.—This play (among other considerations) leads us not to feel much regret that Shakespear was not what is called a classical scholar. We do not think his *forte* would ever have lain in imitating or improving on what others invented, so much as in inventing for himself, and perfecting what he invented—not perhaps by the omission of faults, but by the addition of the highest excellencies. His own genius was strong enough to bear him up, and he soared longest and best on unborrowed plumes.

ETIENNE SOURIAU

from *The Two Hundred Thousand Dramatic Situations*

You may say that the comedy of errors—the mixed-up Menaechmuses in Plautus; Dromio of Ephesus taken for Dromio of Syracuse in Shakespeare; Zerbinetta revealed as the daughter of Argante in *The Tricks of Scapin;*

From *Les Deux Cent Mille Situations Dramatiques* by Etienne Souriau. Paris: Librairie Ernest Flammarion, 1950. Reprinted by permission of Librairie Ernest Flammarion. Translated by the editor.

Valère thinking he has secretly married Lucile while marrying Ascagne, actually a girl disguised as a boy, in *The Loving Spite;* Silvia dressed as Lisette in *The Game of Love and Chance;* the confusions under the chestnut trees in *The Marriage of Figaro;* or Gennaro unaware that Lucrezia Borgia is his mother—how worn-out it all seems! Stratagems of comedy or melodrama, not serious dramaturgy!

I should answer: first remember *Oedipus the King.* The gradual removal of the veils that conceal the true situation, actually present from the beginning, constitutes the very action that brings about all the successive theatrical situations in fatal and terrible sequence: Oedipus, king of a people which suffers without knowing why; Oedipus knowing that some criminal is responsible for this misfortune, yet unaware of his identity and seeking him out; Oedipus identified as that criminal without knowing why; Oedipus aware that he is a foundling, etc., etc. . . .

One of the greatest practical and technical difficulties in the artistic handling of these elements is, of course, that the author, who is in on the secret, and the spectator, who sees and hears whatever is shown to him, must, on the one hand, arrange and, on the other, experience that artistic treatment of ignorances and errors, through a series of imponderables or clever calculations. But these are, or should be, essentially inherent in the situation, as it is lived through by the characters.

How can it be doubted that such a "comedy of errors" or of ignorances is inherent in the internal organization of the life of the human microcosm as presented to us? Theatrical effect, convention, melodramatic device? Certainly not. In any case, who will deny that the condition of human beings, morally speaking, leads them to grope among the shadows and to play blindman's buff with their souls. The danger, in the theater, is to show those souls as too lucid and too sure of themselves, of what they are doing, and of their situation, rather than to show them as too wild and uncertain, proceeding by trials and errors. It is for the demiurge of this little world to be certain of what he is doing and of where he is going or taking us—and not for those who are going along.

BERTRAND EVANS

from *Shakespeare's Comedies*

To describe the creation, maintenance, and exploitation of the gaps that separate the participants' awarenesses and ours in *The Comedy of Errors* is almost to describe the entire play, for in his first comedy Shakespeare came nearer than ever afterward to placing his whole reliance upon an arrangement of discrepant awarenesses. This comedy has no Falstaff, Toby Belch, Dogberry—not even an Armado. Comic effect emerges not once from character as such. If the Dromios prove laughable, it is not in themselves but in the incompleteness of their vision of situation that they prove so. Language, which regularly afterwards is squeezed for its comic potential, here serves chiefly to keep us advised of situation. Here are no malapropisms, dialectal oddities, few quirks and twists of phrase: the very pun, hereafter ubiquitous, is scanted. With neither character nor language making notable comic contribution, then, the great resource of laughter is the exploitable gulf spread between the participants' understanding and ours.

This gap is held open from beginning to end: it is available for exploitation and is exploited during ten of the eleven scenes. In the course of the action we hold an advantage in awareness over fifteen of the sixteen persons—Aemilia alone never being exhibited on a level beneath ours. Not until *The Tempest* (in the comedies) did Shakespeare again hold one gap open so long for exploitation; never again did he place so great a responsibility on a single gap.

From *Shakespeare's Comedies* by Bertrand Evans. Oxford: The Clarendon Press, 1960. Reprinted by permission of The Clarendon Press.

As in most later plays, Shakespeare here opens the gap
—that is to say, raises our vantage point above that of
the participants—as soon as possible. After forty lines in
Scene ii (at the entrance of Dromio of Ephesus) the facts
of the enveloping situation are fixed in our minds: a
father, facing death unless he can raise money by sunset,
his twin sons, long separated, and their twin servants are
all in the city of Ephesus. But the key fact that is quickly
revealed to us is denied them: they are ignorant that all
are in the same city. On our side, thus, is complete vision,
and on theirs none at all. This condition, kept essentially
unchanged, is made to yield virtually all of the comic
effects during ten scenes.

In that the secret committed to our keeping is both
simple and single, *The Comedy of Errors* is unique among
the comedies. In later ones our awareness is packed, often
even burdened, with multiple, complex, interrelated se-
crets, and the many circles of individual participants'
visions, though they cross and recross one another, do not
wholly coincide. In *Twelfth Night,* thus, certain but not
all facts of the intricate situation are known to both Sir
Toby and Sir Andrew, and some are known to Sir Toby
but not to Sir Andrew; a few, but only a few are shared
by Viola and Sir Toby; some are known to Viola alone
of the participants; and one fact of enormous significance,
known to us alone, is hidden even from Viola. In *The
Comedy of Errors* only a single great secret exists, which
is ours alone; the participants, therefore, stand all on one
footing of ignorance. Shakespeare never again used so
simple an arrangement of the awarenesses.

The enveloping situation which makes both action and
comic effects possible is itself static; it remains unchanged,
until the last 100 lines, by the bustling incidents that fill
up the scenes between beginning and end. Between the
point midway in the second scene, at which all relevant
facts have been put into our minds, and the ending, we
neither need nor get additional information in order to
hold our one great advantage over the participants. The
many expository devices by which Shakespeare was later
to sustain the advantage given us in the initial exposi-
tion—as soliloquies and asides strategically placed, scene

introductions which shed special light on following action, confidential dialogue of persons perpetrating some "practice" on their unwitting fellows—are here absent because they would be superfluous. For whereas in later comedies situations emerge, swell, and multiply, generating new ones to replace the old, so that repeated injections of fact are needed to keep our vision clearer and wider than the participants', in *The Comedy of Errors* the first situation holds firm, unaffected by the frantic activity which it contains. The play has not one "aside," and though there are brief soliloquies they exist not to advise us of what we had been ignorant but to exploit the speaker's ignorance of what we already know.

The Comedy of Errors is unique also in that its exploitable gap between awarenesses is created and sustained throughout the play without the use of a "practicer." No one here willfully deceives another or even passively withholds a secret—for none here knows enough of the situation to deceive others about it, and none has a secret to withhold. In later comedies, some "practice," some form of deliberate deception, is foremost among the means by which Shakespeare creates discrepancies in awareness and is prominent also among the means by which he maintains or widens these. Moreover, in all the later plays in which exploitation of discrepancies is of primary importance, the role of the deceiver is also of primary importance; that is to say, in plays that show a high proportion of scenes in which most participants perceive the situation less clearly than we do, this high proportion is typically the result of the presence and activity of one or more willful practicers. Many of these practicers—in the histories and the tragedies especially—are of a villainous turn, or are outright villains, whose practices on their fellows are wicked. In *Richard III* the huge proportion of scenes which exploit participants' ignorance of their situations owes largely to Richard's secret machinations; in *Titus Andronicus,* to those of Aaron and Tamora; in *Othello,* to those of Iago; in *Much Ado About Nothing,* to those of Don John; in *Cymbeline,* to those of Iachimo. But not all the practicers who serve the dramatist well by opening exploitable gaps between the awarenesses of participants and audience are vicious. There are far, far more "good" than "bad" practicers in Shakespeare's plays, and accordingly more scenes of unawareness are acted under a benign light than under a sinister shadow. For Rosalind is no less a "practicer" than Iago; and Bassanio's Portia, Viola, Helena, and Imogen deceive even as do Edmund and Iachimo, and by deceiving open gaps between other participants' awarenesses and ours. Hamlet stands high among the notable benevolent practicers, along with Oberon, Duke Vincentio, and many others, all looking ultimately to Prospero.

With the roles of "practicers" it will be necessary to be much concerned hereafter—and with the differences in dramatic effect when, on the one hand, the highest point of awareness among the participants is occupied by a benevolent or, at worst, a sportive practicer and, on the other, when it is held by a vicious one. Frequently the truth that is hidden from the persons of a scene is worse than they suspect; often it is better than they dream. Nearly always, it is the nature of the practicer that determines. Nevertheless, though his role is conspicuous in most plays, the practicer is but one of several means used by the dramatist to create differences between awarenesses. And the fullest evidence that a play can rely for its effects almost exclusively on exploitation of such differences and yet get along without any deceiver, either benevolent or wicked, is presented by *The Comedy of Errors*. If Antipholus of Syracuse deceives Adriana by looking like his brother, yet he does not do so deliberately, and he is himself deceived by Dromio of Ephesus, who looks like Dromio of Syracuse. And if Dromio of Syracuse deceives by resembling his brother, yet he is simultaneously deceived because Antipholus of Ephesus looks like Antipholus of Syracuse. None who deceives in this play is aware that he deceives. None perceives the truth clearly enough to try to deceive another about it.

In fact, none sees the truth at all, or guesses anywhere near it. The third distinguishing mark of *The Comedy of Errors,* seen from the point of view of its uses of awareness, is the universal depth of the participants' ignorance. In later plays persons ignorant of a situation occasionally glimpse the truth, even though dimly and obliquely, and the effect is an instant flash of irony. So, for example, in *Twelfth Night,* the Duke at once sees and sees not when, speaking to the loving "Cesario," he asserts that "thine eye/Hath stay'd upon some favor that it loves." And, in tragedy, Romeo, entering the Capulet house, expresses misgivings of "some consequence yet hanging in the stars" —and his hit on the truth told us in the Prologue is recorded by a flash. But no person in *The Comedy of Errors* ever rises enough from the bottom of oblivion to glimpse the truth that we see steadily. In the first lines of Scene ii, the First Merchant mentions a fact which—if he but knew—would be enormously significant to Antipholus of Syracuse: "This very day a Syracusian merchant/Is apprehended for arrival here." And he goes on:

> And, not being able to buy out his life
> According to the statute of the town,
> Dies ere the weary sun set in the west.
> There is your money that I had to keep.
>
> (I.ii.5–8.)

Without a word about the plight of the "Syracusian merchant," Antipholus takes the money—the very sum that would buy his father's life—and turns to instruct his servant. The intellectual remoteness of Antipholus from a truth that physically brushes against him at the outset of the action is matched constantly thereafter by the remoteness of other participants from truth that assaults their eyes and ears, and escapes detection. In his first use of the method, Shakespeare risks no dialogue that strikes the unsuspected truth. Nor, certainly, does he allow any participant to come close to guessing the truth. In *Twelfth Night,* after her encounter with the officers taking Antonio to jail, Viola's quick mind accurately interprets the incident: "Prove true, imagination, O, prove true,/That I, dear brother, be now ta'en for you!" There are no such moments in *The Comedy of Errors;* here Shakespeare keeps all persons safely oblivious. Though truth beats at them incessantly, it beats in vain.

C. L. BARBER

from *Shakespearian Comedy in "The Comedy of Errors"*

Shakespeare's sense of comedy as a moment in a larger cycle leads him to go out of his way, even in this early play, to frame farce with action which presents the weight of age and the threat of death, and to make the comic resolution a renewal of life, indeed explicitly a rebirth. One must admit, however, that he does rather go out of his way to do it: Egeon and Emilia are offstage and almost entirely out of mind in all but the first and last scenes. We can notice, however, that the bonds of marriage, broken in their case by romantic accident, are also very much at issue in the intervening scenes, where marriage is subjected to the very unromantic strains of temperament grinding on temperament in the setting of daily life. Moreover, Adriana and her Antipholus are both *in* their marriage (as wooing couples are in love); its hold on them comes out under the special stress of the presence of the twin doubles. The seriousness of the marriage, however trying, appears in Adriana's long speech rebuking and pleading with her husband when he seems at last to have come home to dinner (it is, of course, the wrong brother):

From "Shakespearian Comedy in *The Comedy of Errors*," by C. L. Barber. *College English*, XXV (April, 1964), 493–97. Reprinted by permission of the National Council of Teachers of English and C. L. Barber.

Ah, do not tear thyself away from me;
For know, my love, as easy mayst thou fall
A drop of water in the breaking gulf,
And take unmingled thence that drop again, . . .
As take from me thyself and not me too.
How dearly would it touch thee to the quick,
Shouldst thou but hear I were licentious . . .

That for her husband home and wife are really primary is made explicit even when he is most angry:

Since mine own doors refuse to entertain me,
I'll knock elsewhere, to see if they'll disdain me.

Shakespeare nowhere else deals with the daily substance of marriage, its irritations and its strong holding power (*The Merry Wives of Windsor* touches some of this, at a later stage of married life; the rest of the comedies are wooing and wedding). There *is* a deep logic, therefore, to merging, in the ending, the fulfillment of a long-stretched, romantic longing of husband and wife with the conclusion, in the household of Antipholus, of domestic peace after domestic frenzy. No doubt their peace is temporary, but for the moment all vexation is spent; and Adriana *may* have learned something from the Abbess' lecture, even though the Abbess turns out to be her mother-in-law!

LOUISE GEORGE CLUBB

Italian Comedy and *The Comedy of Errors*

T. W. Baldwin's latest word on the compositional
genetics of *The Comedy of Errors* accounts exhaustively
for every single gene, and not one is Italian. Nevertheless,
Professor Baldwin states that Shakespeare's comedy is
"probably the most fundamentally Italianate play of the
English lot, and yet there is not a specific element which
can be traced to direct borrowing from the Italian," adding in a note:

> It must be evident to anyone who has grasped this devel-
> opment of the type in England that so skillfully compli-
> cated a play as *Errors* could not have been constructed
> before the end of the 'eighties. Even so, it is as remark-
> able a personal accomplishment for the late 'eighties as
> Udall's *Ralph Roister Doister* was for the early 'fifties. I
> have the impression that this point of evolution would be
> stronger if it were put on the background of the develop-
> ment in Italy of this more complicated form from the
> simpler form of Plautus and Terence.[1]

Whether this impression, with its apparently subversive
effect on the rest of the book, is inserted merely as a
protective clause to appease Italianists, only Professor
Baldwin can say. But his suggestion is very much worth
taking, though it touches on the sore old question of

We reprint a portion of an essay originally published in *Comparative
Literature*, 19 (1967), 240–51.
[1] *On the Compositional Genetics of The Comedy of Errors* (Urbana,
1965), p. 208.

whether or not Italian Renaissance comedy exercised any significant influence on the Elizabethan drama, especially Shakespeare's.

There are only a few proved connections to support Stephen Gosson's famous complaint that Italian comedies were "ransackt to furnish the Playe houses in London." Some comedies of Ariosto, Grazzini, Aretino, the Intronati, Salviati, Piccolomini, Pasqualigo, Della Porta, and Oddi were translated or adapted in England. From the late 1570s, Italian comedy was decidedly chic at Cambridge, where Latin versions were frequently performed. Both of Machiavelli's and four of Aretino's comedies were printed in London in 1588. Royal interest in "Comedia Italiana" is proved by Queen Elizabeth's request that her courtiers organize a performance of one. There are records of seven visits to England of Italian players between 1546 and 1578, and by 1591 the traffic seems to have been brisk enough to make disguise as Italian entertainers desirable to foreign spies.[2]

But despite the handful of undisputed facts, as despite the analogues recorded by several generations of scholars, the investigation of the Elizabethan debt to Italian comedy has been stymied by the scarcity of documentary proof of physical contact or direct borrowing, and by the distractions of the common raw materials, notably Latin comedy and *novelle*.

With regard to Shakespeare the question is especially tantalizing, for half his plays smack of Italian drama, none more than *The Comedy of Errors*. It is generally agreed that the sources of *The Comedy of Errors* are a combination of *Menaechmi* and *Amphitruo,* Gower's version of Apollonius of Tyre, and the account of St. Paul's travels in The Acts of the Apostles, that Shakespeare's handling is more complex than Plautus', and that the whole is given a serious turn, a touch of spirituality and of horror. It is customary to add that Shakespeare raised the moral tone, cleaned up the meretrix, introduced topics of marriage

[2] K. M. Lea, *Italian Popular Comedy, II* (Oxford, 1934), 362–363 and 352 ff.

courtship, and providence, and developed the themes of madness and sorcery—indeed, Professor Baldwin calls the latter the "chief structural thread."

The Italianate quality of *The Comedy of Errors* has never been met head on. K. M. Lea will not commit herself beyond the suggestion that Shakespeare "seems to have been acquainted with the way the comedy of mistaken identity was exploited on the Italian stage" and points to parallels between the devices for moving and complicating action in *The Comedy of Errors* and those in *commedia dell'arte* scenarios. Other scholars consider the style of *The Comedy of Errors* a derivation of Gascoigne's and Lyly's ventures into Italianate comedy, attributing the leftover differences to Shakespeare's desire to outcomplicate *Mother Bombie*. Even M. C. Bradbrook, who distinguishes between the "English Plautine" *Mother Bombie* and the "Italian Plautine" *Comedy of Errors,* does not come to grips with the Italian tradition or with the way in which *The Comedy of Errors* is linked to it.[3]

* * *

It will be noticed that except for certain commonplaces of situation, the plots of the plays used as examples of *commedia grave* do not resemble that of *The Comedy of Errors*. The time of searching for Shakespeare's immediate sources is past. There are many Italian regular comedies based on *Menaechmi,* but there is no reason to suppose that Shakespeare used any of them or to doubt that his sources were Plautus, Gower, and St. Paul. His choice of elements and his way of blending them, however, give pause. The addition of pathos and hint of tragedy; the moral de-emphasizing of the courtesan's role to play up the wife Adriana and her nubile sister; the dialogue of these two on the topos of jealousy in marriage; the weaving of multiple sources into a newly complicated pattern of errors with something like a unifying theme in the thread of feared madness and sorcery; Aegeon's evaluation of "the gods" at the beginning, proved false at the

[3] *The Growth and Structure of Elizabethan Comedy* (London, 1955), p. 66.

end, when the maddening errors and nearly fatal sentence
become instruments to reunite families and confirm loves:
the combination of these elements, characteristic of *commedia grave,* could not have been suggested by Lyly or
Gasciogne, for both *Mother Bombie* and *Supposes* belong
to the earlier type of regular comedy.

While Geoffrey Bullough recognizes that Shakespeare's
addition of pathos and tragic import to his source was
anticipated by "some of the Italians," he still accepts E. K.
Chambers' statement that Shakespeare was "consciously
experimenting with an archaistic form," and he adds,
"the remarkable thing is the complexity he wove within
the simple outline provided by Plautus' *Menaechmi.*"[4] But
examining *The Comedy of Errors* against the background
of Italian tradition, as Baldwin suggests, reveals that the
form is anything but archaistic. The complexity answers
the demands of Italian regular comedy in general, and the
character of its unity reflects the *commedia grave* in particular. As for the pathos and tragic import, they are not
fortuitously anticipated by "some" Italians, but were
deliberately developed by a sizable group of conscious
artists representing the avant-garde of the day.

It cannot be proved that Shakespeare read Italian plays,
or saw *commedia dell'arte* troupes or Italian amateurs at
Elizabeth's court perform *commedie gravi,* or heard about
them from a friend. Nor can *The Comedy of Errors* be
labelled *commedia grave,* for Shakespeare's most Italianate play is still not an Italian one. It is next to certain,
however, that the brilliant young upstart crow knew something about the latest Continental fashion in comedy.

[4] *Narrative and Dramatic Sources of Shakespeare* (London, 1957),
pp. 10, 3, 5.

The Comedy of Errors on Stage and Screen

This may seem the slightest of Shakespeare's plays; certainly it is the very shortest, with no more than 1,787 lines. Yet it has enjoyed "a considerable life on the stage," as one of its many adapters, Thomas Hull, attested in 1764; and the continuing history of its performance has been at least as rich and eventful as that of those first 170 years. Its relative slightness seems, increasingly, to have invited elaboration. Its modest and marginal place in the Shakespearean canon stimulated ingenuity and licensed innovation on the part of its successive producers. Here was "a play which blushes at no experiment," in the words of the actor-director-critic, Robert Speaight. Paradoxically, it was also Shakespeare at his most traditional, since it had retained close ties with its Latin sources and had paid its respects to the classical unities, though the jocose Plautine model had been far from constraining. In keeping with that tradition, it has a long record of amateur presentation under more or less academic auspices. But, given the rapidity of its timing, the neatness of its dialogue, and the agility of its twists and turns, *The Comedy of Errors* has never ceased to attract the most professional talents.

Its *donnée,* the gimmick of the identical twins, would have been much easier to present in the Roman theater, where the actors wore masks. Unmasked actors, only roughly resembling each other in physique and physiognomy, had to rely as best they could on costume and makeup, plus a willing suspension of disbelief. Shakespeare had compounded the mixups of the *Menaechmi* by redoubling his doubles, but his pair of twins held a compensating advantage for their audience: while it would be less plausible to confuse them, it would be less difficult to tell them apart. It was an exceptional circumstance that could recruit two comedians who were brothers, Charles and Henry Webb, to play the complementary Dromios during the mid-nineteenth century. Certain modern productions, like the one at Stratford, Connecticut, in 1963, have sought to resolve the dilemma by casting dual roles, with a single actor as the two Antipholi and another as both Dromios. This is an expedient which ends by creating as many dilemmas as it resolves, since direct confrontation must be avoided and stand-in mutes employed to blunt the recognition scene. Needless to say, the technique of double exposure can effectually eliminate such problems, when the medium is film.

Farce derives its name from a French word for stuffing; literally it welcomes the gags and the knockabout business that fill in its contours *ad libitum*. More broadly speaking, it is structured by surprises, which in turn depend upon improbable situations, all too frequently upon coincidence. Spectators need not worry too much about what goes on, if events move fast and emotions do not go very deep. Accordingly, plot flourishes at the expense of characterization, more than elsewhere in Shakespearean drama, since the precondition for the two main sets of characters is that they should be nearly indistinguishable. Such reduplication does nothing to bolster leading roles, and it is not surprising that actor-managers tended on the whole to stay away. John Philip Kemble included the play in his repertory during the early years of the nineteenth century, and emphasized its more sentimental discomfitures—those glimpses of later Shakespeare through Egeon and Adriana —but without much popular success. Sybil Thorndike would make her debut at the Old Vic as Adriana in the Ben Greet production of 1915. Alfred Lunt, starting out at the age of twenty with Boston's Castle Square stock company in 1913, was not above appearing as the Second Officer.

With so short and unified a script, the staging could be

basic in its simplicity, and conveniently suited to court-yards and refectories. The characters keep moving back and forth along a city street, the classic ambience for comedy, which could have been conventionally denoted by the ancient proscenium (a facade with several door-ways) or by the multiple scene of the Middle Ages (a progression from one *domus,* or symbolic "mansion," to the next). Shakespeare's Folio text sets the scenes by repeated reference to specific locations: the Phoenix (home of the Ephesian Antipholus), the Porpentine (abode of the Courtesan), and the Priory (rallying point for the grand finale). This could have been stylized, and even signalized by placards, at three entrances to the Eliz-abethan stage. The text in *Bell's British Theatre,* used by Kemble, specified an integrated background, "A public place," while some productions made the most of unlocal-ized screens or curtains. If place can be unitary, time is continuous, covering about six hours—from mid-morning to mid-afternoon—of one busy day. The concise dramatic action has occasionally suffered further abridgment to fit in with double bills. Thus it counterbalanced Milton's *Comus* on an outdoor program at Regent's Park in 1934.

Our earliest recorded mention of *The Comedy of Errors* occurs in the *Gesta Grayorum,* a vivid first-hand account of the festivities at Gray's Inn during the Christmas season of 1594. Lawyers' headquarters, the Inns of Court were the cultural centers of London; they prided themselves on their courtly entertainments, and had been the formative sponsors of English tragedy a generation before. Now, after three or four years when the plague had shut down their annual celebration, the members of Gray's Inn had invited their legal colleagues from the Inner Temple to a grandiose sequence of nightly revels: feasting and dancing, allegorical pageantry, Latin orations written by Francis Bacon. On Innocents' Night (December 28) their great hall became so crowded and tumultuous that the official ceremony was broken off, the Templarian guests went home, the scheduled "inventions" by the hosts were called off, and Shakespeare's company was called in to furnish the evening's entertainment. ". . . And after such sports," writes the chronicler, "a Comedy of Errors (like to Plautus his *Menaechmi*) was played by the Players. So that Night was begun, and continued to the end, in nothing but Confusion and Errors, whereupon it was ever afterwards called *The Night of Errors*."

We do not know whether that was the play's premiere, or whether it had been publicly produced during the previous year or so; but it seems well chosen to embellish a special occasion under private auspices, and has been generally counted as Shakespeare's initial comedy: Its broad title, which so soon became a proverbial phrase for confusions or mistakes of any kind, might—like *As You Like It* or *All's Well That Ends Well*—have been affixed to virtually any comic plot. Later adaptations likewise seem to have opted for generalizing titles: *Every Body Mistaken* (1716), *See If You Like It* (1734), *In Such a World* (1935). Gray's Inn was to witness a tercentenary revival in 1895 by the Elizabethan Stage Society under the direction of William Poel, an effective part of his campaigns for a return to the original conditions of Shakespeare's staging. Arnold Dolmetsch furnished an appropriate consort of Renaissance music. Bernard Shaw, who consistently supported Poel's amateur group as part of his own campaigns against histrionic professionals like Sir Henry Irving, wrote a strongly enthusiastic review. This production should win "the palm of the season," he pointedly declared. It was "a delightful, as distinguished from a commercially promising, first night."

The play had celebrated a much earlier anniversary when, just ten years after that bewildering "night of errors" at Gray's Inn, it was presented at court before the new king, James I, on Innocents' Day, 1604. We know that it continued to be in the active repertory during the Restoration, since a promptbook has survived that once belonged to what was then called "the Nursery," a recruiting ground and training school for the two licensed theatrical companies:

> Where unfledged Actors learn to laugh and cry,
> Where infant Punks their tender voices try—

so Dryden would rather harshly sum up their apprentice efforts. There was, moreover, an acting version among the archives of the Smock Alley Theatre in Dublin during the last years of the seventeenth century, though we have no record of its performance. A transcript of "The Famous Comedy of Errors," dating from 1694 and preserved in the French library at Douai, which was an expatriate center for English Catholics during their years of persecution at home, would seem to suggest that the famous comedy had been locally revived by students at the English-speaking college. It was represented less faithfully in England, during the early eighteenth century, by adaptations heavily reworked.

But Shakespeare's own version (more or less) reentered the repertory at Drury Lane in 1741, and figured as a staple at Covent Garden from 1770 onward. This does not mean that the play no longer posed its standing invitation to would-be adapters with minds of their own. A highly farcical three-act *rifacimento* by William Woods, *The Twins, or Which is Which?*, introduced at the Theatre Royal in Edinburgh, was published in London in 1780 and ran in the provinces through the following generation. As interest in Shakespearean drama spread to the Continent, further modulations and extensions could be looked for. In 1786, shortly after the world premiere of Mozart's *Marriage of Figaro* in Vienna, the Austrian court could listen to another new opera entitled *Gli Equivoci* (a sophisticated Italian rendering of "the errors"). Both works had the same accomplished librettist, Lorenzo da Ponte, who had read *The Comedy of Errors* in a recent French translation. The new composer, designated in German as *"ein Engländer,"* was Stephen Storace, youthful scion of an Anglo-Italian musical family. It almost seems inevitable that a scenario with such symmetrical rhythms and choric climaxes, such potential duets and vocal ensembles, should sooner or later be set to music.

An elaborate musical version in English was mounted at Covent Garden in 1819, composed by Sir Henry Bishop to a libretto by Frederick Reynolds. The original occupied a fairly unusual position among Shakespeare's comedies in that it had contained no lyrics whatsoever. The prolific Bishop, who was to turn out about seventy works for the stage, including other operas of Shakespearean inspiration, is chiefly remembered today for a single song: "Home, Sweet Home." His *Comedy of Errors* is really a kind of ballad-opera, augmented not only with his melodies but with tunes from Mozart, Thomas Arne, and still others. In order to draw upon these contributions Reynolds had spun out the story line, and more than made up for its absence of musical interludes, by somehow working in the drinking scene from *Antony and Cleopatra* and such other numbers as the willow song from *Othello,* "When Icicles Hang by the Wall" from *Love's Labor's Lost,* "Tell Me Where Is Fancy Bred" from *The Merchant of Venice,* and even excerpts from the *Sonnets.* Contemporaries seem to have admired this olio for its songs, score, and spectacle— admired it in spite of the plot, which "was of course absurd, but . . . was borne by the audience for the sake of the music."

Succeeding generations of producers seem to have oscil- lated between imposing radical alterations, on the one hand, and reverting to something like the playwright's intentions on the other. By 1855 the actor-manager Sam- uel Phelps was seeking to redeem the Shakespearean text when he staged it among his revivals at Sadler's Wells. Benjamin Webster, who produced it several times through those middle years, took a straightforward approach, play- ing out the continuities in a curtained space without inter- ruption. He himself played Antipholus of Syracuse; but if there was an increasing tendency to build up a stellar part, it was that of the Syracusian Dromio. Stuart Robson came to star in the comedy during that period, repeating his lines with a habitual squeak but renewing his twin- partners, while enlarging his American productions on a more and more spectacular scale. Picturesque tableaux were interpolated; the narrated shipwreck was dramatized as a prologue; Amazons joined Bacchantes in a *corps de ballet*; a procession for the tutelary goddess, Diana, re-created her second-century Ephesus in archeological detail. Alfred Thompson, the scenic artist of Irving's Lyceum, had been specially commissioned to design the settings and to sketch the more than two hundred costumes requisitioned for the cast.

Influenced perhaps by the development of the cinema, where so many different components—both artistic and technical—must be brought together and synthesized by one responsible individual, our century has seen the emergence of a director's theater. *The Comedy of Errors,* which is not dominated by any actor but requires the coordination of many within some sort of integrating conception, lends itself to this method of stagecraft with particular adaptability. Thus Max Reinhardt was compared to a puppet master for his Berlin production of 1911, where the stage consisted largely of a bridge, with ships on one side, houses on the other, and puppetlike actors rushing up and down. Theatrical traditions, which had crystallized with the touring companies in Britain and other English-speaking countries, were centralized at Stratford-on-Avon under the leadership of F. R. Benson and subsequently William Bridges-Adams. After the old Victorian play-house had burned down, the present Memorial Theatre was built and inaugurated, looming above its riverside gardens vast and nondescript, yet open to directorial and scenic experimentation. An important transition was marked in the nineteen thirties, when the innovative Russian director, Theodore Komisarjevsky, was entrusted with the reinterpretation of six plays.

Never having directed Shakespeare before, Komisarjevsky could announce to the press, "I am not in the least traditional." His scenery, an Italianate or Mediterranean "toytown," was in itself by no means unconventional; yet it centered upon a clock tower that burlesqued the temporal theme by chiming the wrong hours and whirling its hands at irregular intervals. "Time itself joined in the

sport," commented one reviewer. There was a pantomime
by way of induction, with a hurdy-gurdy to supply the
sound effects. Dialogue was vocally orchestrated; some of
the speeches were broken up and passed from mouth to
mouth, while others were pronounced by several speakers
in choral unison. Costumes varied widely in colors, styles,
and periods, though most of the men wore Chaplinesque
bowler hats. Amid a welter of contemporary allusion, the
actress portraying the Courtesan was costumed and made
up to resemble Mae West. In undertaking to deconstruct
the standardized treatment of Shakespeare, it was shrewd
of Komisarjevsky to pick *The Comedy of Errors* as a test
case; for there were not many critics who would insist
upon a strict construction or be put off by high-spirited
improprieties. That constituted, for better and for worse,
a breakthrough.

Its date, 1938, proved to be an *annus mirabilis,* since
the most popular adaptation, *The Boys from Syracuse,*
burst forth upon Broadway in that same year. This musical comedy, one of the happiest collaborations between
the vibrant scores of Richard Rodgers and the colloquial
lyrics of Lorenz Hart, was paced by the assured direction
of George Abbott and enhanced by the brilliant choreog-
raphy of George Balanchine. Its outstanding mime was
the wistful Jimmy Savo, paired with the lyricist's brother
Teddy as his fellow Dromio, while Eddie Albert and
Ronald Graham carried on tunefully at the more debon-
aire level of the Antipholi. Songs like "This Can't Be
Love" and "Sing for Your Supper" still resonate with
nostalgic echoes for many. One of these collaborators
justified the distance from Shakespeare's language on the
grounds that it permitted them to escape the puns. Of all
the elements in their joint concoction, their title was the
last and hardest to pick out. At length they offered a prize
for the best suggestion. Among the also-ran alternatives
were *The Shakespeare Follies, The Bard's Last Stand, It's
About Time, The Face Is Familiar,* and—not excluding
puns—*Twin Feature, Double Trouble, Two to Go,* and
Wherefore Art Thou Dromio?

The selected title must have evoked an extra reverbera-
tion in New York ears: the slightly condescending awareness that newcomers from upstate had recently arrived in
the big town. This reverses the Shakespearean situation,
where Syracuse is the offstage metropolis and Ephesus the
exotic outpost. But it may help to explain why *The Boys
from Syracuse* met with so indifferent a reception at
Drury Lane in 1962—all the more indifferent because it
had been preceded there by the pseudo-Shavian evocation
of London in *My Fair Lady*. As for *The Comedy of
Errors* itself, Komisarjevsky's was a hard act to follow,
and it would not be restaged at Stratford for twenty-four
years. In the meantime (1957), cut down to one fast-
talking hour, it divided the billing with *Titus Andronicus*
at the Old Vic. These two plays made an extreme but
interrelated contrast; both were thinly rooted in the early
classicism that would be guiding Shakespeare from apprenticeship toward mastery: "Seneca cannot be too
heavy, nor Plautus too light." Tragedy and comedy were
both set in an Elizabethan inn yard and performed, as it
were, by a troupe of strolling players. The most notable
performer was the dancer Robert Helpmann as Doctor
Pinch, one of those bit parts which expands into comical
flourishes.

The first post-Komisarjevsky production at Stratford-
on-Avon happened through a lucky accident. What was
now the Royal Shakespeare Theatre had scheduled *King
Lear*, a more traditionally Stratfordian vehicle, when its
principal actor became indisposed. At the last moment
Clifford Williams "knocked together" a *Comedy of Errors*
which was adjudged to be surprisingly "solid and intricate," which would go on to re-create for London viewers
"a Pirandello world of masquerade," and which would
culminate in a command performance before the royal
family at Windsor. More precisely, the Italian atmosphere
was that of the commedia dell' arte; on a bare stage the
cast appeared in black tights for an introductory parade,
and those who were not directly involved would wander
in and out of the dramatic action. At the British Stratford

there have been subsequent revivals. Trevor Nunn's, a decade later (1972), reached the widest audience after it had been filmed and televised. John Napier's (1976), coming so soon afterward, tried hard to divagate: with a fragmented text, a contemporary setting, a middle eastern dictator as duke, and a courtroom scene for the resolution. Adrian Noble (1982), dressing most of his characters as clowns, seems to have turned back to the harlequinade.

When Shakespearean themes could be reanimated with such far-out variations in the mother country, it could be expected that they would be pressed even farther in North America, through a series of cultural syntheses which blended the indigenous with the imported. First brought to the New York theater by a traveling English company in 1804, the play reappeared very frequently throughout the nineteenth century. A pioneering black group, The Ethiopian Art Theater, took it from Chicago and Washington to Broadway for two precarious weeks (1923) in an updated production "à la jazz"—according to W. E. B. Du Bois, whose article protested against the snobbery that was keeping his fellow blacks away from the classics. Ideological tensions between the rival towns became a major issue with Players, Inc., a group of strollers whose version featured crowds with signs reading "Ephesus for Ephesians" and "Syracusans Go Home" (1959). *The Comedy of Errors* has been a regular favorite in the *al fresco* program of Joseph Papp's New York Shakespeare Festival in Central Park. In its most striking incarnation (1975), Italy was noisily projected as it might have been in the far-from-romantic nineteen thirties; the Duke was a Mafioso, guns went off, and actors spoke with Italian-American accents.

Meanwhile (again in 1975), Elizabethan affairs were conveyed much closer to home by the Canadian Shakespeare Festival in Stratford, Ontario. Robin Phillips' musicalized rendition was relocated in the American West during the latter nineteenth century. The Duke—in order to meet that contingency—was a rancher, surrounded by cowboys and adept at presiding over square dances. The *decor* was a farmyard, complete with drying laundry and clucking chickens, and centering on a prairie schooner. At this juncture we have come a long way; we are closer to *Oklahoma!* here than to the urban conventions of ancient comedy. If the aims were modernization and naturalization, it would have been more appropriate to transmute the *dramatis personae* into types encountered along the midway of a carnival. Consequently, in the Shakespeare Festival in Ashland, Oregon (1976), the Antipholi were enacted as animal tamers, the Dromios as a team of clowns, and Doctor Pinch as a medicine man, while the Priory was reduced to a funhouse. Under the same sponsorship six years later, a renovated *Comedy of Errors* added a Harpo Marx personage known as "the Kid"—as if there were not enough interlopers already. The critics' complaint, that too many pies were thrown, might apply more widely.

When each revision strives to outdo the very latest, there can be no limits. To date the uttermost endeavor has been that of five acrobatic zanies who—traducing Dostoyevsky along with Shakespeare—bill themselves as the Flying Karamazovs (originally at Chicago's Goodman Theater in 1983, then in New York and on television in 1987). Four of them accounted for the dual twins; the fifth personified Shakespeare himself, not speaking but laughing continually at his own jokes; a sixth comedian supplemented their muggings as an eccentric janitor; and Adriana twirled the baton of a drum majorette. Ephesus, reconceived this time as the winter quarters of a circus ("three-ring Shakespeare"), could thus play host to an uproarious vaudeville of acts on stilts, trapezes, and tightropes, of tap dancing and belly dancing, of unexpected incursions by unicycles and kiddy cars. A program note explained: "The plot has something to do with twins and jugglers," evidently taking off from the Shakespearean warning against "nimble jugglers that deceive the eye." But juggling, for Shakespeare, did not necessarily mean tossing tenpins into the air; it was a byword for trickery in a more general sense, with overtones of deception, and was etymologically connected with joking.

Latitude had to be broadened even further, when Shakespeare's dramas were transposed to the audiovisual media, but if this raised technological complications, it opened up fresh possibilities. It was all too obvious that *The Comedy of Errors,* "because of its reliance upon intractably visual material," was uniquely unsuited to aural dramatization via the radio. Yet its peculiar visual requirements, at best imperfectly realized on the stage, were readily adaptable to the film through the use of composite shots. Both Dromios could look just like Joe Penner, and both Antipholi like Allan Jones, with the Courtesan looking like no one but Martha Raye, when *The Boys from Syracuse* was screened in 1940. The play itself, not reaching the cinema houses except through its musical popularization, would be repeatedly filmed for the television screens. It was rather gradual in adjusting to, and expanding with, the new medium. The main concern was for the Royal Shakespeare Company to be televised by the British Broadcasting Corporation. There would be unquestionable value in recording, disseminating widely, and ultimately preserving such interpretations, notably that of Clifford Williams. But the effect on home viewers could be too "stagey"; some of them felt that Trevor Nunn's production was "overdirected" (1976).

Conversely and more lately, when the BBC undertook to range through the whole Shakespearean sequence, it was ready to reconsider the drama in terms of the camera; and its *Comedy of Errors* (1984), as directed by James Cellan Jones, with Cyril Cusack as Egeon and Wendy Hiller as Emilia, turned out to be one of its most suggestive reenactments. Freed from platform or proscenium, the photographer made the most of spaciousness and mobility; a map of the Mediterranean was laid out underfoot in mosaic as a dancing-place for the players, a counterpart of the Greek *orchestra*. But the observer's vision could move, in a flash, from the distancing of a long shot to the intimacy of a close-up: a pair of clasped hands, a pack of Tarot cards. Monologues could begin full-face and proceed through a *montage* of associations. Whereas the inherited convention had dwelt upon externals, the streets and the façades, there was now a psychological impulse to penetrate interiors. When visualization can be linked with characterization, and characters can be regarded through one another's eyes, their blunders and their bafflements assume a deeper dimension. A brittle farce, modulated by shifting viewpoints, takes on the characteristics of a novel.

It could scarcely have been predicted that so comparatively slight a play, so limited and formalized at its beginnings, would have so colorful a history and so worldwide a diffusion. Not only did it have a place in the universal adoption of Shakespeare's works into other languages and cultures, but it more than held its ground among them. Mikhail Morozov designates fourteen Shakespearean plays that currently belong to "'the basic repertory" of the Soviet Russian theater; his list includes *The Comedy of Errors,* though it omits *Macbeth, Julius Caesar,* and *The Tempest.* Naturally, performance in distant regions was bound to be colored by native tastes and customs. We have had occasion to notice several instances of high-pressured Americanization. Comparably a Swahili rendering, performed by the National Theater of Kenya (1955), was enlivened by African folk-dances. It seems clear enough that we are dealing with a thematic structure which, while lending itself to all kinds of incidental embellishment, firmly persists across regional and historical change. This principle was already established when Shakespeare found stimulus in Plautus, who had hit upon an important archetype: the question of identity and otherness, the self and the *alter ego,* the haunting apparition of the Double.

Plautus had dashed off the outlines lightly and brightly. Shakespeare would not have been himself, even in the course of his earliest comic undertaking, if he had not darkened the Roman picture with Elizabethan touches of *chiaroscuro*: the overarching suspense of Egeon's plight, the feminine pathos of Adriana's dilemma—not to mention the providential resurgence of Emilia as *dea ex machina*. The resultant mingle-mangle has allowed great leeway to its dramatic interpreters, who may choose to stress the more serious aspects or else to fall back upon the farcical substructure. That ambivalence, reinforcing the plotted ambiguities, made it easier to interpolate more freely. There have been frequent reactions in favor of Shakespeare's well-made script; hence this brief chronicle has had to veer between the minimalist presentation and the jazzed-up extravaganza. It has been a long time now since critics objected to the play on grounds of improbability; doubtless their afterthoughts reflect a shift from presumptions of stability and rationalism toward a state of mind where confusion comes closer to social norms. At all events, it is heartening that Shakespeare can still speak to an age of existential absurdity, and that his comedy of errors can vie with those of Beckett and Ionesco for distinction in the Theater of the Absurd.

Bibliographic Note. Accounts of major productions are cited mainly from standard histories of the London and the New York stage. Reports from all over the world that continue from year to year can be found in both the annual *Shakespeare Survey*, going back to 1948, and the *Shakespeare Quarterly*, starting from 1950. The first production on record is analyzed by Margaret Knapp and Michael Kobialka in "Shakespeare and the Prince of Purpoole: The 1594 Production of *The Comedy of Errors* at Gray's Inn Hall," *Theatre History Studies*, 4 (1984). Robert E. Wood considers the most up-to-date version in "Cooling the Comedy: Television as a Medium for Shakespeare's *Comedy of Errors*," *Literature/Film Quarterly*, 14, 4 (1986).

Suggested References

The number of possible references is vast and grows alarmingly. (The *Shakespeare Quarterly* devotes one issue each year to a list of the previous year's work, and *Shakespeare Survey*—an annual publication—includes a substantial review of recent scholarship, as well as an occasional essay surveying a few decades of scholarship on a chosen topic.) Though no works are indispensable, those listed below have been found especially helpful.

1. Shakespeare's Times

Byrne, M. St. Clare. *Elizabethan Life in Town and Country*. Rev. ed. New York: Barnes & Noble, 1961. Chapters on manners, beliefs, education, etc., with illustrations.

Joseph, B. L. *Shakespeare's Eden: The Commonwealth of England, 1558–1629*. New York: Barnes & Noble, 1971. An account of the social, political, economic, and cultural life of England.

Schoenbaum, S. *Shakespeare: The Globe and the World*. New York: Oxford University Press, 1979. A readable, handsomely illustrated book on the world of the Elizabethans.

Shakespeare's England. 2 vols. London: Oxford University Press, 1916. A large collection of scholarly essays on a wide variety of topics (e.g. astrology, costume, gardening, horsemanship), with special attention to Shakespeare's references to these topics.

Stone, Lawrence. *The Crisis of the Aristocracy, 1558–1641*, abridged edition. London: Oxford University Press, 1967.

2. Shakespeare

Barnet, Sylvan. *A Short Guide to Shakespeare*. New York:

Harcourt Brace Jovanovich, 1974. An introduction to all of the works and to the dramatic traditions behind them.

Bentley, Gerald E. *Shakespeare: A Biographical Handbook.* New Haven, Conn.: Yale University Press, 1961. The facts about Shakespeare, with virtually no conjecture intermingled.

Bush, Geoffrey. *Shakespeare and the Natural Condition.* Cambridge, Mass.: Harvard University Press, 1956. A short, sensitive account of Shakespeare's view of "Nature," touching most of the works.

Chambers, E. K. *William Shakespeare: A Study of Facts and Problems.* 2 vols. London: Oxford University Press, 1930. An invaluable, detailed reference work; not for the casual reader.

Chute, Marchette. *Shakespeare of London.* New York: Dutton, 1949. A readable biography fused with portraits of Stratford and London life.

Clemen, Wolfgang H. *The Development of Shakespeare's Imagery.* Cambridge, Mass.: Harvard University Press, 1951. (Originally published in German, 1936.) A temperate account of a subject often abused.

Granville-Barker, Harley. *Prefaces to Shakespeare.* 2 vols. Princeton, N. J.: Princeton University Press, 1946–47. Essays on ten plays by a scholarly man of the theater.

Harbage, Alfred. *As They Liked It.* New York: Macmillan, 1947. A long, sensitive essay on Shakespeare, morality, and the audience's expectations.

Kernan, Alvin B., ed. *Modern Shakespearean Criticism: Essays on Style, Dramaturgy, and the Major Plays.* New York: Harcourt Brace Jovanovich, 1970. A collection of major formalist criticism.

————. "The Plays and the Playwrights." In *The Revels History of Drama in English,* general editors Clifford Leech and T. W. Craik. Vol. III. London: Methuen, 1975. A book-length essay surveying Elizabethan drama with substantial discussions of Shakespeare's plays.

Schoenbaum, S. *Shakespeare's Lives.* Oxford: Clarendon Press, 1970. A review of the evidence, and an examination of many biographies, including those by Baconians and other heretics.

————. *William Shakespeare: A Compact Documentary Life.* New York: Oxford University Press, 1977. A readable presentation of all that the documents tell us about Shakespeare.

Traversi, D. A. *An Approach to Shakespeare.* 3rd rev. ed. 2 vols. New York: Doubleday, 1968–69. An analysis of the plays beginning with words, images, and themes, rather than with characters.

Van Doren, Mark. *Shakespeare.* New York: Holt, 1939. Brief, perceptive readings of all of the plays.

3. Shakespeare's Theater

Beckerman, Bernard. *Shakespeare at the Globe 1599–1609.* New York: Macmillan, 1962. On the playhouse and on Elizabethan dramaturgy, acting, and staging.

Chambers, E. K. *The Elizabethan Stage.* 4 vols. New York: Oxford University Press, 1945. A major reference work on theaters, theatrical companies, and staging at court.

Cook, Ann Jennalie. *The Privilgeed Playgoers of Shakespeare's London, 1576–1642.* Princeton, N. J.: Princeton University Press, 1981. Sees Shakespeare's audience as more middle-class and more intellectual than Harbage (below) does.

Gurr, Andrew. *The Shakespearean Stage: 1579–1642.* 2d edition. Cambridge: Cambridge University Press, 1980. On the acting companies, the actors, the playhouses, the stages, and the audiences.

Harbage, Alfred. *Shakespeare's Audience.* New York: Columbia University Press, 1941. A study of the size and nature of the theatrical public, emphasizing its representativeness.

Hodges, C. Walter. *The Globe Restored.* London: Ernest Benn, 1953. A well-illustrated and readable attempt to reconstruct the Globe Theatre.

Hosley, Richard. "The Playhouses." In *The Revels History of Drama in English,* general editors Clifford Leech and T. W. Craik. Vol. III. London: Methuen, 1975. An essay of one hundred pages on the physical aspects of the playhouses.

Kernodle, George R. *From Art to Theatre: Form and Convention in the Renaissance.* Chicago: University of Chicago

Press, 1944. Pioneering and stimulating work on the symbolic and cultural meanings of theater construction.

Nagler, A. M. *Shakespeare's Stage*. Trans. Ralph Manheim New Haven, Conn.: Yale University Press, 1958. A very brief introduction to the physical aspects of the playhouse

Slater, Ann Pasternak. *Shakespeare the Director*. Totowa N. J.: Barnes & Noble, 1982. An analysis of theatrica' effects (e.g., kissing, kneeling) in stage directions and dialogue.

Thomson, Peter. *Shakespeare's Theatre*. London: Routledge & Kegan Paul, 1983. A discussion of how plays were staged in Shakespeare's time.

4. Miscellaneous Reference Works

Abbott, E. A. *A Shakespearean Grammar*. New edition. New York: Macmillan, 1877. An examination of differences between Elizabethan and modern grammar.

Bevington, David. *Shakespeare*. Arlington Heights, Ill.: A. H. M. Publishing, 1978. A short guide to hundreds of important writings on the works.

Bullough, Geoffrey. *Narrative and Dramatic Sources of Shakespeare*. 8 vols. New York: Columbia University Press, 1957–75. A collection of many of the books Shakespeare drew upon, with judicious comments.

Campbell, Cscar James, and Edward G. Quinn. *The Reader's Encyclopedia of Shakespeare*. New York: Crowell, 1966. More than 2,600 entries, from a few sentences to a few pages, on everything related to Shakespeare.

Greg, W. W. *The Shakespeare First Folio*. New York: Oxford University Press, 1955. A detailed yet readable history of the first collection (1623) of Shakespeare's plays.

Kökeritz, Helge. *Shakespeare's Names*. New Haven, Conn.: Yale University Press, 1959. A guide to the pronunciation of some 1,800 names appearing in Shakespeare.

————. *Shakespeare's Pronunciation*. New Haven, Conn.: Yale University Press, 1953. Contains much information about puns and rhymes.

Muir, Kenneth. *The Sources of Shakespeare's Plays*. New Haven, Conn.: Yale University Press, 1978. An account of Shakespeare's use of his reading.

The Norton Facsimile: The First Folio of Shakespeare. Prepared by Charles Hinman. New York: Norton, 1968. A handsome and accurate facsimile of the first collection (1623) of Shakespeare's plays.

Onions, C. T. *A Shakespeare Glossary.* 2d ed., rev., with enlarged addenda. London: Oxford University Press, 1953. Definitions of words (or senses of words) now obsolete.

Partridge, Eric. *Shakespeare's Bawdy.* Rev. ed. New York: Dutton, 1955. A glossary of bawdy words and phrases.

Shakespeare Quarterly. See headnote to Suggested References.

Shakespeare Survey. See headnote to Suggested References.

Shakespeare's Plays in Quarto. A Facsimile Edition. Ed. Michael J. B. Allen and Kenneth Muir. Berkeley, Calif.: University of California Press, 1981. A book of nine hundred pages, containing facsimiles of twenty-two of the quarto editions of Shakespeare's plays. An invaluable complement to *The Norton Facsimile: The First Folio of Shakespeare* (see above).

Smith, Gordon Ross. *A Classified Shakespeare Bibliography 1936–1958.* University Park, Pa.: Pennsylvania State University Press, 1963. A list of some twenty thousand items on Shakespeare.

Spevack, Marvin. *The Harvard Concordance to Shakespeare.* Cambridge, Mass.: Harvard University Press, 1973. An index to Shakespeare's words.

Wells, Stanley, ed. *Shakespeare: Select Bibliographies.* London: Oxford University Press, 1973. Seventeen essays surveying scholarship and criticism of Shakespeare's life, work, and theater.

5. *The Comedy of Errors*

Brooks, Harold F. "Themes and Structure in *The Comedy of Errors*," *Early Shakespeare: Stratford-upon-Avon Studies* 3. London: Edward Arnold, Ltd., 1961.

Brown, John Russell. *Shakespeare and His Comedies.* London: Methuen, 1957.

Charney, Maurice (ed.). *Shakespearean Comedy.* New York: New York Literary Forum, 1980.

Fergusson, Francis. "Two Comedies," *The Human Image in Dramatic Literature.* Garden City, N.Y.: Doubleday, 1957.

Foakes, R. A. (ed.). *The Comedy of Errors: The Arden Edition of the Works of William Shakespeare.* Cambridge, Mass.: Harvard University Press; London: Methuen, 1962.

Grivelet, Michel. "Shakespeare, Molière, and the Comedy of Antiquity," *Shakespeare Survey* 22. Cambridge: Cambridge University Press, 1969.

Salgādo, Gāmini. " 'Time's Deform'd Hand': Sequence, Consequence, and Inconsequence in *The Comedy of Errors*," *Shakespeare Survey* 25. Cambridge: Cambridge University Press, 1972.

Salingar, Leo. *Shakespeare and the Traditions of Comedy.* Cambridge: Cambridge University Press, 1974.

Tetzeli von Rosador, Kurt. "Plotting the Early Comedies: *The Comedy of Errors, Love's Labour's Lost, Two Gentlemen of Verona,*" *Shakespeare Survey* 37. Cambridge: Cambridge University Press, 1984.

Williams, Gwyn. "*The Comedy of Errors* Rescued from Tragedy," *A Review of English Literature,* 5 (October, 1964), 63–71.

Ⓒ SIGNET CLASSIC   (0451)

THE WORKS OF CHARLES DICKENS

*Prices slightly higher in Canada

**Buy them at your local
bookstore or use coupon
on next page for ordering.**

BRITISH CLASSICS

☐ **TYPHOON AND OTHER TALES by Joseph Conrad.**   (009367—$4.50)

☐ **LORD JIM by Joseph Conrad.**   (511956—$1.95)

☐ **NOSTROMO by Joseph Conrad.** Foreword by F. R. Leavis.(520920—$3.95)

☐ **HEART OF DARKNESS and THE SECRET SHARER by Joseph Conrad.**
Introduction by Albert J. Guerard.   (520726—$1.95)*

☐ **FAR FROM THE MADDING CROWD by Thomas Hardy.** Afterword by
James Wright Macalester.   (521153—$2.95)

☐ **JUDE THE OBSCURE by Thomas Hardy.** Foreword by A. Alvarez.
                                                      (517830—$2.95)

☐ **THE MAYOR OF CASTERBRIDGE by Thomas Hardy.** Afterword by Walter
Allen.   (512308—$1.95)

☐ **THE RETURN OF THE NATIVE by Thomas Hardy.**   (523075—$2.50)*

☐ **TESS OF THE D'URBERVILLES by Thomas Hardy.** Afterword by Donald Hall.
                                                      (519248—$2.95)*

☐ **KIM by Rudyard Kipling.** Introduction by Raymond Carney.
                                                      (521447—$2.50)*

☐ **CAPTAINS COURAGEOUS by Rudyard Kipling.** Afterword by C. A. Bodelsen.
                                                      (517512—$1.95)

☐ **THE JUNGLE BOOKS by Rudyard Kipling.** Afterword by Marcus Cunliffe.
                                                      (521927—$3.50)

☐ **JUST SO STORIES by Rudyard Kipling.**   (521803—$2.95)

☐ **KIDNAPPED by Robert Louis Stevenson.**   (519728—$1.95)*

☐ **THE SHERLOCK HOLMES MYSTERIES by Sir Arthur Conan Doyle.**
                                                      (521064—$3.50)

*Price slightly higher in Canada
†Not available in Canada

Buy them at your local bookstore or use this convenient coupon for ordering.

NEW AMERICAN LIBRARY
P.O. Box 999, Bergenfield, New Jersey 07621

Please send me the books I have checked above. I am enclosing $_____
(please add $1.00 to this order to cover postage and handling). Send check or money
order—no cash or C.O.D.'s. Prices and numbers are subject to change without
notice.

Name_____

Address_____

City _____ State _____ Zip Code _____
Allow 4-6 weeks for delivery.
This offer, prices and numbers are subject to change without notice.